"I love this book so muc[h] ... ways burdened me to see a p...... ...., ...,p creating, stop living life to the fullest. God is a Creator God, and we are made in His image. Thank you, Len, for encouraging us to dream again!"
—**Ron Edmondson**, pastor, blogger, church leadership consultant

"I've always believed that everyone is born creative. But there's something about entering the educational system that starts pushing our sense of wonder into the background. Now, Len Wilson shows us how to rediscover our imagination in his amazing new book *Think Like a Five-Year-Old*. Get this book, because after reading it, you'll never look at life's challenges the same way again."
—**Phil Cooke**, filmmaker, media consultant, and author of *One Big Thing: Discovering What You Were Born to Do*

"This remarkable book is for all of us who long to recapture the wondrous creativity we once took for granted. Len Wilson draws from inspiring stories of real people who fought the battle for divergent thinking and practiced the disciplines required to innovate. I highly recommend this practical and inspiring work and plan to give it to my artistic daughters."
—**Nancy Beach**, leadership coach, The Slingshot Group and author of *The Hour on Sunday* and *Gifted to Lead*

"I can't recommend this book strongly enough. Len Wilson's work is not only significant and inspiring but also critical for our society in this time. His insights are perhaps especially important for church leaders as we attempt to discover how to make the gospel message authentic in our ever-changing and isolating landscape. Spirituality and creativity cannot be separated. We all need to be called again to become childlike in our faith, our imagination, and our sense of wonder and possibility that we may recapture the creativity the Creator placed in all of us. This book is for the closet-creative and child in each of us that is just waiting to break free."
—**Gary Rivas**, pastor, Gracepoint Church, Johannesburg, South Africa

"*Think Like a Five-Year-Old* invites us to take a bold, surrendered risk into a more creative, fulfilling life."
—**Rebekah Lyons**, author, *Freefall to Fly*

"Len writes as a man who is both deeply creative and intensely pastoral. In *Think Like a Five-Year-Old*, he dives deeply into the heart of any person who believes that creativity matters. In his thought-provoking and beautiful words, Len is helping us all discover the beauty of being a follower of Jesus and living a creative life that's from the gut. There are people in my life who cannot see the creativity God is calling them to, and they'll be the first people to whom I send this book."
—**Gary Molander**, co-owner, Floodgate Productions, and author of *Pursuing Christ. Creating Art.*

"As someone who pays the bills by creating art, I've found it's easy to get caught up in the industry of production and consumption. I am always on the brink of burnout. Though I love creating moments of wonder and astonishment for other people, I struggle with losing my own childlike wonder. Like me, Len knows this tension all too well. I'm so grateful that he's shared his story of becoming a kid again."
—**Stephen Proctor**, worship artist, illuminate.us

"In a world encumbered with dull and gray, Len Wilson offers us a brilliant, Technicolor future by inviting us to harness our unique, God-given creativity. As creatures made in the image of God, each one of us has untapped ingenuity yet to be expressed. This book is for anyone who wants to tap into this well of imagination."
—**Jorge Acevedo**, lead pastor, Grace Church of southwest Florida, and author of *Vital: Churches Changing Communities and the World*

"If you want to recover some of the wonder you had as a child, then read this book. It will help you discover what you once had—creativity."
—**Bill Easum**, author, consultant, and coach, 21st Century Strategies

"Len Wilson's excellent book isn't just for those who would call themselves 'creative.' It is packed with practical insights to help me grow as a communicator and storyteller. Using these principles, Len has brought creative wonder back into local churches to tell better stories and change more lives."
—**Bryan Dunagan**, senior pastor, Highland Park Presbyterian Church, Dallas

"A plethora of blog posts offer 10 ways to get more creative or 6 ways to find inspiration. Don't look for such facile answers here. Instead, discover a set of rich illustrations and powerful stories that reveals what it really means to drink from the fountain of fulfillment."
—**Joe Carmichael**, pastor, United Methodist Church

"Len Wilson's *Think Like a Five-Year-Old* takes us back to the playground to cultivate renewed habits that lead to new futures. Thoughtful and thought-full, Len dares us to pick ourselves up and dust ourselves off, like a diligent Little Leaguer first learning to swing for the fences. Regardless of where you now believe you are on the creativity spectrum, this book will take you further!"
—**Dr. Jay Richard Akkerman**, Director of Graduate Theological Online Education, Northwest Nazarene University, author of *Missional Discipleship: Partners in God's Redemptive Mission*

"A great watercolorist once said creativity was the convergence of five blessings: contrast, composition, intuition, humility, and effortlessness. Len has painted a book to model these blessings. Once you have read it, then stand at a distance to look at it. Then you will get it."
—**Thomas G. Bandy**, conference speaker, leadership coach, president of Thriving Church Consulting, LLC

THINK
like a
5-YEAR-OLD

RECLAIM YOUR WONDER &
CREATE Great THINGS

LEN WILSON

Abingdon Press

Nashville

THINK LIKE A FIVE-YEAR-OLD
RECLAIM YOUR WONDER AND CREATE GREAT THINGS

Copyright © 2015 by Len Wilson

Library of Congress Cataloging-in-Publication Data
Wilson, Len, 1970-
  Think like a five year old : reclaim your wonder and create great things / Len Wilson.
    pages cm
  ISBN 978-1-4267-8641-9 (binding : soft back : alk. paper) 1. Christianity and the arts. 2. Creation (Literary, artistic, etc.)—Religious aspects—Christianity. I. Title.
  BR115.A8W55 2015
  261.5'7—dc23

2014044836

Scripture quotations unless noted otherwise are taken from the Common English Bible. Copyright © 2011 by the Common English Bible. All rights reserved. Used by permission. www.CommonEnglishBible.com.

Scripture quotations marked (ESV) are from The Holy Bible, English Standard Version® (ESV®), copyright © 2001 by Crossway, a publishing ministry of Good News Publishers. Used by permission. All rights reserved.

Scripture quotations marked (NIV) are taken from the Holy Bible, New International Version®, NIV®. Copyright © 1973, 1978, 1984, 2011 by Biblica, Inc.™ Used by permission of Zondervan. All rights reserved worldwide. www.zondervan.com. The "NIV" and "New International Version" are trademarks registered in the United States Patent and Trademark Office by Biblica, Inc.™

15 16 17 18 19 20 21 22 23 24—10 9 8 7 6 5 4 3 2 1
MANUFACTURED IN THE UNITED STATES OF AMERICA

Therefore, if anyone is in Christ, he is a new creation.
The old has passed away; behold, the new has come.

2 Corinthians 5:17 (ESV)

When you showed me myself I became someone else.

Joseph Arthur

Contents

Contents

A Few Creative Suggestions

Preface

"How is the new job? Will you stay for a bit, or are you getting wanderlust?"

My friend's note bothered me. I looked the word up. Do I have professional wanderlust—an insatiable desire to move from job to job, growing bored and never staying in one place very long? Is it obvious?

A few weeks later I read a statistic from the Gallup people that said only 13 percent of us are "actively engaged" in our jobs.[1] The majority of us—63 percent—merely put in our time at work and go home. According to the same study, the remaining 24 percent of us are actively disengaged. Although we may have been taught from an early age that fulfillment in life comes from naming passions and pursuing dreams (and we may still post nice quotes to that effect on our social networks), we no longer functionally believe it. We may have good educations; we may have decent salaries. But we are bored—at work, at home, in our personal habits, and in our spiritual lives. We don't feel very fulfilled.

Not coincidentally, we also don't feel very creative.

Defining creativity is tricky. Creativity is a means to something; it is not a product or a hard skill. You don't ship creativity; you ship what creativity does. Nonetheless, we have a sense of what *creativity* means. Call someone *creative* and you're probably referring to a certain type of person. Someone with energy. An art lover. A problem solver. Someone with good ideas.

The number one most popular TED talk is on the subject of creativity. In it, the presenter, creativity researcher Sir Ken Robinson, says that creativity is the process of having original ideas that have value.[2]

Paul Torrance, who has been called the father of creativity, says that creativity is a process of becoming sensitive to problems, deficiencies, gaps in knowledge, missing elements, disharmonies, and so on; identifying the difficulty; searching for solutions, making guesses; testing and retesting these hypotheses; and finally communicating the results.[3]

My five-year-old says that creativity is when you have fun and make stuff. He says it's not something he really thinks about. He just does it.

I like my five-year-old's definition best. Creativity includes having original ideas with value, and it includes the process of solving problems. But it is much more. Creativity is life. It's just what we do. We are created not to consume but to create. God's human design is that we would be cocreators.

And what is it that we create? I believe it is art, regardless of our vocation or location. We may be engineers or computer geeks or consultants or housewives or academics, but when we create, we become artists, each in our own way.

Seth Godin, the marketer who has become a leading spokesperson for the networked world of the twenty-first century, says that now, we don't have creative interests or hobbies. In our postindustrial culture, what we used to call a hobby can now become our livelihood, if we have sufficient passion. To some degree, I think Godin makes a living selling the mythology of the Internet, that we can all be rich and famous. Yet I am intrigued with the glimpse Godin gives us of a God-given power and promise that each of us has a creative calling:

> One ghetto that we used to reserve for artists was the idea that they made luxury items, entertainments and objects that had nothing to do with productivity or utility. I think that was convenient but wrong, even fifty years ago. Thomas Edison was a monopolist (and an artist). Henry Ford's slavish devotion to his concept of interchangeable parts and mass production was as much an art project as an opportunity to make money. Madame Curie gave her life to doing the art of real science.[4]

In other words, creativity is not just for people writing sonnets. Each vocation, each professional life can be engaged creatively. But it's even better than that. Godin hints at a truth about creativity. Creativity is about listening to, and living out of, the voice in your inner being—your heart, mind, soul, and strength; in other words, creativity is about being attentive to and acting in response to the combination of ideas and reactions and preferences that form your view of the world. This perspective, this unique form of expression, is the identity given to you by God and the origin of your creativity. We come with it preloaded. We're each born an artist. We're made to be creative. When we, as an image of God, exercise our heavenly impulse, the result of our expression, regardless of our field of endeavor, is art. This power, which reflects the essence of God, reveals itself in the passions we feel.

The problem is that while we have this supernatural power, this creative wellspring, within us, we've lost it. We've given in to forces that would steal and destroy this innate joy. We don't feel creative, and consequently, we don't feel fulfilled.

It's time to counter these destructive impulses, reclaim the art God has designed for us to make, and start creating great things. Maybe, along the way, we can also discover a more fulfilling life.

Part One

I Had It, but I Lost It

1

Trajectory | The Story of Creativity

What will be remembered as the pinnacle of American civilization, when the dust settles in at some future point, will perhaps be two things: the Internet and the moon landing. The moon landing is more remarkable, considering it was powered with the computing power of an alarm clock. What powered the NASA program wasn't technology, but creative ingenuity.

The third manned mission to the moon, Apollo 13, didn't achieve its goal—the astronaut crew endured an on-board explosion and was forced to abort their mission—but it did demonstrate the creative power of the people involved. The explosion had taken the ship's power. The three astronauts were forced to abandon the command module, which is the main hold of the ship, and crowd into the small lunar module. There they realized that the on-board carbon dioxide removal system was built for a crew of two, not three, and for a day and a half reconnaissance trip to the lunar surface, not a four-day haul back to Earth. The astronauts called and reported their carbon dioxide problem to flight control in Houston. They needed more filters. They were becoming hypoxic, losing breathable air, and without a quick solution would pass out and die.

The main command module of the ship had filters, but they were cube-shaped, and the ones on the lunar module were cylindrical. "Tell me this isn't a government operation," said Kranz, played by actor Ed Harris, in Ron Howard's epic film of the experience. But they had no choice. It was their only possible fix. With insufficient round lunar module cartridges, the Houston engineers, in a matter of hours, had to figure out how literally to put a square peg in a round hole, using only parts available on board the ship.

A short time later, the stranded astronauts received a set of instructions from Houston. They named the device they built with the instructions "the mailbox" for its shape and the life-saving materials it delivered.

The kind of creativity that puts a man on the moon doesn't just happen. It's the result of an intentional effort to foster a creative culture. (In fact, to an uncreative world, such feats seem impossible. A poll in 2009 by the British periodical *Engineering & Technology* found that 25 percent of people believe the moon landing was an elaborate hoax, perpetuated on a Hollywood soundstage.[1])

In the buildup to the Apollo 11 mission, a NASA deputy director had approached a researcher named George Land. He had lots of applicants, he said. But measuring people by standard intelligence measures (that is, the conventional IQ test) wasn't sufficient. He needed a way to select the people who would create the best solutions because NASA had unusually tough questions.

NASA's issue wasn't finding intelligent people. Their issue was finding people who could think differently and demonstrate the sort of ingenuity that could solve the sort of problem that plagued the aborted Apollo 13 mission. Land and his team developed an instrument to measure creative thinking, and NASA implemented it as an additional step in their candidate vetting process.

The test was a rousing success and, as a measure of employee performance, highly predictive for NASA. Afterward, a question remained for Land and his research crew. They had determined how to measure existing levels of creative thinking in prospective employees, but that didn't solve more fundamental questions. Is creativity innate, learned, or—perhaps—unlearned?

Since the test questions were simple to understand, they decided to give the same test to a group of young children. They administered it to a sample of sixteen hundred five-year-olds.

The results were astonishing. They learned that 98 percent of five-year-olds were what the NASA test described as "creative genius."

The In Between

George Land and his team of NASA-contracted researchers decided to track their young creative geniuses over time. They turned their research into a longitudinal study and, five years later, retested the same group of students. Among the same group of children, now ten years old, there was a drastic change: only 30 percent were creative geniuses. Again, at fifteen years old, 12 percent were creative geniuses. Throughout the period of the study, and since, Land and his team tested thousands of adults, far past the flat line of statistical analysis. They learned, with an average age of thirty-one years old, that 2 percent of adults are creative geniuses.[2]

In their famous study, Land and his team not only solved an important issue facing NASA leadership but also discovered a fundamental problem—one that plagues business, education, culture, and the life of faith.

Each of us was once a creative genius.

Somewhere along the way, though, we lost it—not entirely but to a significant degree. We may not be complete creative dolts. We can match an entree with a side dish, we can sometimes figure out when our phone's GPS is lying to us, we can choose among twenty flavors of stationery at the store, and, if pressed, we can actually contribute an idea at a business meeting. But we're far from what you'd call a creative genius.

As a creative director, I hear people apologize for the lack of creativity all the time. It's sometimes their lead sentence: "Oh, I'm not very creative." We like to refer to a "creative person" as some sort of special species possessing rare talent. We see ourselves as somewhere in between.

The archetypal image of creativity is the garage. Larry Page and Sergey Brin (Google), Jeff Bezos (Amazon), Steve Jobs (Apple), The Who, Nirvana, Walt Disney, Harley and Davidson, Hewlett and Packard—entire industries share the same opening scene of young, hungry rule breakers working out of their garage. Because of this, we think of the metaphor of the garage as the setting for innovation and the seed for great things.

The thing is, most of us no longer tinker in our garage. Most of us don't even own a garage anymore. Instead, we own an attached storage shed. One study revealed that 75 percent of American garages are so filled with clutter that they have no room to store an automobile.[3] Instead of metaphors for creativity and innovation, our garages have become final resting places for the artifacts of our consumption.

Perhaps circumstances dictate our choices; perhaps we become impatient with waiting and uncertainty. When we party on the weekend or get away after work with music and a drink with friends, maybe what we're doing is trying to regain our soul because all day we've been trading it in for a paycheck.

I don't want to work,
I want to bang on the drum all day.

—Todd Rundgren

The problem isn't that most of us are incapable of creativity. Land's study and other scientific studies disprove the false dichotomy of creatives versus noncreatives. Creativity recovery isn't a switch to turn on, and to find our creative self doesn't mean we must drag the lake of our psyche, although this may be something you're inclined to do. Rather, creativity can be nurtured and developed. When we make the unexamined declaration that we are not creative, as most of us do, we rob ourselves of a powerful means of knowing and experiencing God's work in our lives.

Land's study is a scientific insight for what I believe is primarily a spiritual issue. We've lost our ability to create.

This book isn't for the 2 percent of adults who are still actively engaging their creative genius all the time. This book is for the 98 percent—those of us who are former creative geniuses and those of us who want to recover the creativity and the sense of joy and engagement we have lost.

The Source

One way of thinking about the way we have distanced ourselves from creativity is this; we have lost sight of our creativity's source. As creatures made in God's image, we are designed by God to be like God, and this means we're designed to create, not peripherally but as part of our fundamental nature. In other words, in the beginning, we are each given, as part of the warranty of being human, a harmonic calling, the melody of a set of good things to do with our lives. As an image or representation of God, when we create, we reflect the character of God and the glory of God. Our God-given creative passion is our unique art and the source of our fulfillment.

For the artist there is no distinction between work and living. His work is his life, and the whole of his life.

—Dorothy Sayers[4]

Each of us is made to be God's cocreator. And, as with any creative process, the work draws the workers together. When we create, we move closer to God; conversely, when we merely consume, we move further from God. To call someone, or yourself, uncreative is simply untrue. Our creativity problem is not that we don't have this supernatural power within us. It's that we have lost track of it. It's latent.

8

I believe that when we seek to become more creative, we're really seeking to rediscover our unique art. God intends, through the grace of faith in Christ, to re-create us: to reintroduce us to our identity as God's creatures. When we reclaim this original creativity, we become who we were made to be, whole and complete: images of God. Creativity and faith are kindred spirits. When we follow Christ, we become a new creation. And when, out of the wonder of this recovered identity, we create, our fulfillment and God's glory happen at the same time, and the result is great things that hopefully play a part in changing the world.

To be clear, this rediscovery isn't necessarily religious. Often, it's not. As Romans 1 points out, all of creation points to the glory of God. In other words, creativity can be those things Robinson and Torrance said—new ideas and solved problems. It can be a new look to a designer, a better solution to an engineer, an alternate strategy to an executive, a more organized calendar for a mom, or "adding value" to a business plan. Creativity builds, not destroys. It answers a question, helps someone, or expresses an idea. In all of these activities, when we create, we make wonder, to ourselves and to others who benefit from our work.

> *Creativity is not a luxury. It is essential for personal security and fulfillment.*
>
> —Sir Ken Robinson[5]

Most creative people have maintained, and relearned, a way of thinking (a philosophy), a discipline of living (a strategy), and a set of tactical practices that help them to do what they do. These are not sacrosanct; indeed, we the 98 percent can learn them, increase our creativity, and rediscover our art. I believe there is a high correlation between rediscovering our creativity and overcoming a lack of engagement in our work and in our life. This book is about helping you find the melody of passions that is God's accomplishment in you.

We are God's accomplishment, created in Christ Jesus to do good things. God planned for these good things to be the way that we live our lives.

—Ephesians 2:10

The goal of this book is to help you know the story of your creativity: why you had it to begin with, how you lost it, and how to get it back. Each of us is called to a life of creativity: to know how we are made, to reclaim our passion, to learn the craft of creativity as an act of faith, and to surrender this act to God. My hope is to help propel you back to a trajectory of creativity. A creative life is fulfilling, productive, often successful, and usually harmonious—the kind of life we want.

How do we reclaim the wonder we're made to make? In order to understand creativity let's first turn to the group of people who get it best: children.

2

Storyboard | Five Ways Children Understand Creativity

I assure you that if you don't turn your lives around and become like this little child, you will definitely not enter the kingdom of heaven.

—Matthew 18:3

Preproduction

Recently I interrupted a film preproduction meeting in my entryway. With four children, I never know what I am going find when I get home. On this day they'd apparently written a complete screenplay (which I was not allowed to see) and were discussing how to film it. They'd decided the best way to storyboard the script was to crowd-source: each child drew up interpretations of select scenes from the script, mounted it on a large piece of plywood, and, one by one, pitched the vision to the group. The group then decided which storyboard to shoot for each scene.

Of course, you say. Kids are creative. A regular joke that circulates among young parents at bounce-house parties is the desire to steal whatever creative-life-force-high-energy drug children are on. Kids are full of life and wonder. They're growing. They embody the creative spirit. We want all these things as grownups.

But just because children are creative, and we were once children, doesn't mean that we are automatically creative or gain their creativity by osmosis. In fact most days being around children is intensely counterproductive. Yet, I have found that being around children somehow increases my creativity.

Here is a set of tips I have learned from my children.

Things My Children Have Taught Me About Creativity

1. "What If" Questions

I love to ask my kids crazy questions at the dinner table. One night I asked them to give advice to their younger brother on starting his kindergarten year: what is one thing you wish you'd known that will help him? They all shared tips, and I learned some things about their life and how they think. Sometimes I'll lead a sentence with "What if . . .?" For example, I'll say, "What if we had to make a new product to sell using only this straw and that roll of masking tape? What could we make?" They generate amazing ideas. After a period of brainstorming, I'll ask them which idea they think might sell the best on the shelf at the department store. Besides having lots of fun, I am trying to maintain their natural "what if" thinking, which we innately possess but lose as we age.

"What if" thinking is a well-known principle of creativity. It is the kind of thinking that CEOs desperately want in themselves and in their organizations. It's the ability to think with a new mind about an existing problem, to use limited resources for new application. As the Apollo 13 engineers were forced to do, "what if" thinking encourages new solutions to seemingly impossible problems.

"What if" thinking is more properly known as divergent thinking. Ironically, though this trait is highly desired in business and cultural life, our schools don't teach it well, if at all. If you grew up going to Sunday school, perhaps like me, you learned quickly that the safest and most probable answer to any question was simple: Jesus. In our schools, companies, and churches, we teach convergent thinking, or at least it happens naturally and we don't stop it. We learn from an early age not to say whatever comes to mind, but to say what we perceive is correct. We learn to look for a single, definitive answer when often the problem has multiple answers.

2. Fearlessness

In a family of people in touch with creativity, my eldest daughter may lead the way. She is fearless and given any sort of blank canvas will immediately begin creating. While in a summer musical theater camp before her sixth-grade year, she volunteered to do some set pieces. She brought home some paints and commandeered the space where my truck parks—yes, the garage. She spread out a massive cardboard wall and, with her younger sister, painted it white and added in a house with windows, signs, flowers, and so on. She made an entire scene, without sketching it out first or worrying that she had no backup paint or second massive piece of cardboard

13

should she screw up. She didn't even know that what she was doing was an act of bravery. She just wanted to draw.

3. Space for Chaos

The downside to my daughter's ability to instantly convert any space into a studio is that she doesn't yet know the concept of a blank canvas. Everywhere she goes in our house, and especially when she includes her siblings, she trashes the place. In the space of a few hours, my entryway was full of stuff, and after their pre-production meeting, no studio intern came and cleaned up. For the weeks she painted her set pieces, I couldn't park in my garage.

Writing this, I sound pathetic. Why should I care? Let my children create. It's just that, with ten rooms in our house, at any given time eight or nine of them are trashed. It seems while we clean one, they trash another with creative verve. Without squelching their creative spirit, I have been trying to teach my children that there's a time for creating and a time for doing the more mundane work of preparing and cleaning. So far they're not buying it.

I'll admit, I'm a clean-desk guy. I like a blank canvas to start the day. A blank canvas gives me both the feeling of possibility—I am unencumbered with past or concurrent projects—and the satisfaction of having accomplished something prior, which results in a clear desk. The problem is that sometimes I let my desire for order get in the way of actually doing things. I tend to obsess. As a result I have had to create structure around my workday. For example, I used to obsess at having an empty e-mail inbox, until I discovered that there's a poor correlation between true productivity and having read and replied to every e-mail sent to me.

I like order. Just as I'm teaching my daughter that there's a time for cleanup, she's reminding me that there's a time for chaos, too.

4. Immediacy

If you're a parent, you've perhaps experienced the Now phenomenon. Mini people without calendars are free to indulge their every interest. It goes something like this:

> Son: Dad, can we build the model car now?
>
> Dad: Yes, soon, but right now I'm doing our bills.
>
> Son: Can we do it today?
>
> Dad: I don't know yet.
>
> Son: Please! I really want to do it!
>
> Dad declines to answer. Five minutes pass.
>
> Son: What about now? Can we go now?

Kids don't wait around. They live in the moment. While highly irritating to a grown-up trying to get something completed, a child's immediacy is a form of initiative or courage. They don't consider what they do work, because they don't see a downside. They have an idea, and they move on it. They want to have fun and make stuff.

I've learned a lot by observing this. Creative inspiration appears at inconvenient times, when I am busy with something else. I used to push it away as something to get to later. As an adult, I don't have the freedom to live in the moment. I have a schedule. Big mistake. Most of us lose this sense of immediacy, and it kills our creativity. Inspiration doesn't wait around.

5. Honesty

My nine-year-old son started a blog. I suppose he'd become inspired by my own blog experiment. He was fascinated with my blog

15

software's back-end tracking data and the idea—still amazing, even to a digital-age child—that hundreds of people from around Earth could instantly read something that I'd written. He wanted his own analytics account and tracking system. I told him he needed to post something first.

And post he did. After two months, he'd posted over twenty times.

One day my father called and alerted me to a problem. I logged on and discovered that my son had just told the world about a private conversation we'd had. It seems he'd taken my injunction to be honest to heart and, in the course of writing a post about ideas that might become good business plans, had revealed the specific price I'd sold a share in a business for—not only the kind of thing you want to avoid advertising but also a clear violation of the terms of agreement and something that could have gotten me in hot water.

I immediately told him to remove the offending sentence and that future posts would need to be approved by me. His post count dropped precipitously after my approval system went into effect.

I hated having to institute an approval system because I knew what was going to happen. Rather than have to run everything through me, he just quit posting. It's the same thing that happens to each of us—in our families, our marriages and intimate relationships, our jobs, our public lives. An invisible approval system hangs over our work, preventing us from ever taking on the work at all.

This is how we learn to bury honesty and accept dissonance.

It's not that we learn to lie, though this happens. Instead, we learn to hide our honest thoughts because of the potential side effects. (Honesty: may lead to migraine headaches, sleep loss, sleep apnea, stress-induced fever, muscle pain, heart disease, and death.) Most of us aren't honest because we can't afford it. Unfortunately by my own hand, my son had learned how to keep his honest thoughts to himself—that to reveal what he was thinking would get him in trouble with his father and grandfather.

This is to some degree inevitable. We can't very well improve our social standing by blurting out every thought, like Jim Carrey's truth-telling character in *Liar, Liar*. But the problem with self-censorship is that, in order to maintain the tension, we end up burying the true thought, so that in the end, we have deceived ourselves into believing the untruth, or at least pretending the truth isn't there. We become unable to distinguish between the raw, honest material of our minds and the polished ingot our social filters produce. We skip right to the ingot. We learn to immediately evaluate every idea based on its perceived reception.

This becomes very difficult to unlearn. Even though my son revealed some personal information, I tried to tell him that's okay and to write down his honest thoughts and not worry about results, but to simply come to me between the honest thoughts and the finished post. Unfortunately, people hear this type of advice all the time, but it's almost impossible to live out. We learn to immediately evaluate. There are too many pressures and competing demands in our personal atmosphere.

It's not a coincidence that at the time this happened, my son was a nine-year-old fourth-grader. I was witnessing the fourth-grade slump, which is what happens when we begin to lose our creativity.

3

Wonder Free | How, Somewhere Along the Way, We Lose It

I always knew this altogether thunder
was lost in our little lives.

—REM, "Sweetness Follows"

A Creativity Story

Mark Twain was tired of the "slavery of pen and paper." After seven difficult years of labor, he had published *Adventures of Huckleberry Finn*. But Finn's author didn't want to write anymore.

Twenty years earlier, as a Missouri newspaper journalist, Samuel Clemens achieved his first national success with an article titled "The Celebrated Jumping Frog of Calaveras County." At the time (perhaps like our current time) journalism had a tenuous relationship with objective, detached truth telling. Twain was interested in telling truth, not necessarily facts, and used his journalistic craft as a platform for commentary on society. His resulting satire got him in

19

trouble on more than one occasion. He rode a late-night rail out of Hannibal, Missouri, to avoid a duel challenger, and later he did the same thing to avoid the threats of San Francisco policemen for his portrayal of their treatment of immigrant Chinese.

Twain had the mind of a five-year-old. He understood the necessity of being honest. From San Francisco he traveled to the Sandwich Islands (which we now call Hawaii), writing all the while, and when he returned, he launched what is perhaps the first modern (and literal) American example of what digerati call "having a platform": the Sandwich Islands lectures, in which he regaled audiences with fascinating and hilarious stories of adventures in exotic lands. Twain performed on dozens of stages across the West and worked from a self-made business plan. He even did his own marketing, with pithy poster copy:

Doors open at 7½; the trouble will begin at 8.

—Mark Twain

It was a fabulous success. By the time he was thirty years old, he'd become a national phenomenon. With the success of the Sandwich lectures, doors opened. He became acquainted with eastern establishment society. He pursued and eventually won the hand of a wealthy merchant's daughter. He settled in Hartford, Connecticut, and for a decade and a half, beginning with his marriage at age thirty-five and lasting until he reached fifty, Twain lived in a sweet spot of home and creative life.

During this period, Samuel Clemens channeled his pen name and alter ego, Mark Twain, to write some of the greatest works of American literature, including *The Adventures of Tom Sawyer*, *The Prince and the Pauper* and *Adventures of Huckleberry Finn*. It was a period of amazing productivity and matched his period of greatest personal fulfillment, when Clemens lived and worked at home with his wife and three young girls.

But there was a parasitical downside to his personal golden age.

Clemens enjoyed his celebrity, and, as football coach Bill Parcells has been known to say, "ate the cheese," or gave in to the delicious mousetrap of glory. His lifestyle grew to gargantuan proportions. At his peak, Clemens was spending $30,000 annually on household expenses—the rough equivalent of $750,000 today. He held elaborate parties at his home and basked in his own celebrity.

As the benefits of success grew, Clemens discovered his ability to create became more challenging. Following the overwhelming success of *Tom Sawyer*, he wrote what many critics described as a "safer" novel, *The Prince and the Pauper*, which perhaps reflected his newfound acceptance in eastern elite society.

Next came the sequel to *Tom Sawyer*, which was a difficult creative mountain to climb. He had many false starts and at one point set the project aside for years to pursue business ventures, perhaps due not only to the challenge of his craft but also to the pressure to live up to what he'd previously achieved. He was becoming distracted.

One of his ventures was his own publishing company. (Any writer who has watched the majority of financial return from his or her words go to other parties understands his motivation.) His publishing company met with early success, releasing what was at the time the best-selling book in American history, Ulysses S. Grant's memoirs.

Fascinated with new technology, Clemens was a classic early adopter. His was the first residence in town to put in a telephone. He saw the potential of mechanical innovation and, buoyed by Grant's memoirs, invested in what was to be a revolutionary typesetting machine for his company and, he hoped, the entire printing industry.

In spite of these distractions, Clemens found his creative muse on a trip to his boyhood home. He returned to writing and completed *Adventures of Huckleberry Finn*, the masterpiece epitomized by many as the "great American novel."

But with its completion, he was exhausted. He announced he was retiring from writing—"the slavery of pen and paper." He had obligations to support and businesses to nurture. He focused on the more linear work of making money and maintaining his position in society.

Yet his income couldn't keep pace with the expenses he'd created for himself. His typesetting machine, the Paige Compositor, became an obsession. He poured tens of thousands of dollars into it. It refused to function reliably, and he could neither use it nor convince any major newspaper or printing company to use it. Meanwhile his publishing company couldn't find another manuscript like Grant's memoirs and began to lose money.

Clemens had other business ideas that failed, too, but worst of all was the compositor. The longer it failed to meet his investment, the more he poured into it. It became his Powerball ticket, his hydrant to extinguish rising debt. But it refused to work. Within five years, by age fifty-five, Samuel Clemens filed for bankruptcy and suffered great personal tragedy with the death of his youngest daughter.

In spite of his troubles, he clung to the failed promise of the compositor. His lawyer set him up with one final demonstration, at the *Chicago Tribune*. It failed to convince buyers. In the end, he had invested more than $300,000 into the machine, the equivalent of $8 million today. The only thing it had composited was his money, into wisps of unfulfilled distraction.

Clemens had fallen prey to the demons of creativity.[1]

Fourth-Grade Slump

"It is, perhaps, education's Bermuda Triangle. For decades, educators have wrung their hands over a puzzling phenomenon that often occurs at around age 9 or 10: Students who were previously doing well in school see their performance dip, sometimes permanently."[2] Educators such as Bryan Goodwin are familiar with an infamous drop in performance in late elementary school called the fourth-grade slump. Paul Torrance, often called the father of creativity, and others have documented the drop extensively. It can happen anywhere from third through fifth grade and is characterized by an increased hesitancy to take risks, a loss of spontaneity, less playfulness, and a general decline in creativity.

Sir Ken Robinson, a leading spokesperson on creativity, says the current education system squeezes creativity out of people, and the fourth-grade slump is the consequence of full assimilation into a complex network of learning that begins at kindergarten. Robinson is certainly not wrong; our Western scientific legacy rewards the convergence of a final answer more than the divergence of exploration. But there's more at play than just the science of problem solving. There are psychological and spiritual powers at work, and I believe they start around fourth grade, at an age of rising self-awareness. Many of us stop being creative at this time because we realize it's easier to shut down self-expression than deal with other people's negative opinions and reactions. We self-inhibit.

Most of us have no idea how to "uninhibit." By the time we leave elementary school, we've developed a morbid fear of rejection and have shut off our own imagination.

The Venn Between

One day I stumbled upon a Venn diagram posted by an artist named Peder Norrby into the digital ether. After tweeting it, and with several days thinking about it, I realized it was quite profound. In one circle he'd posted words of self-affirmation. In the other circle were words of self-criticism. In the overlapping space where the circles met lived the word "creativity." His Venn diagram captures something about what happens when we lose wonder: the ability to create it and eventually the ability to even recognize it.

A little later I read an excellent book on the creative process called *The War of Art* by Steven Pressfield. Ostensibly it's for "creatives," which means it's for everyone, because each of us as part of the 98 percent has latent creativity, and a type of art to make, and each of us struggles with making it. Pressfield gives a name—Resistance—to the forces inside each of us that keep us from doing what we are meant to do. When we attempt to exercise our God-designed creative calling, we meet Resistance.

Resistance seems to come from outside ourselves. We locate it in our spouses, jobs, bosses, kids. "Peripheral opponents," as Pat Riley used to say when he coached the Los Angeles Lakers. Resistance is not a peripheral opponent. Resistance arises from within.

—Steven Pressfield[3]

We go looking for scapegoats for our unrealized aspirations. The real problem isn't other people but a gravitational pull from some other, deeper source that draws us to the extremes of self-affirmation and self-criticism; we'll use "I stink" and "I rock." The extremes aren't necessarily bad; in fact, at points they are necessary. Each is critical to the creative process. If you skip "I rock," then you never experience the courage you need to see something through. We drown in our own limitations.

What if they find out I'm not really a prince?

—Aladdin

However, if you skip "I stink," you never experience the humility that leads to the self-examination that all great work requires. Creative people know this is the road that lay ahead of every great work. If you only live in the middle, your art shows it: tepid and bland. The thing that prevents much work from reaching its potential is that we shy away from the journey because we know it's hard.

Here is the challenge: we can't stay at one extreme or the other. We must eventually return to the Venn between.

The Internet Venn diagram and Pressfield's resistance are different ways of describing the inhibition that steals our creativity. These are safe terms. I instead use the term *demons*, which may seem like hocus-pocus or an overdramatic term to use. But, although I don't refer to cartoon characters on my shoulder, I believe the word *demon* is accurate because it's what happened to Jesus, and it is how we lose our creativity.

4

Demons | The Lies That Steal Our Creativity

Perhaps Jesus is not the first person who comes to mind when you think of creativity. Yet, at the least, aside from any belief in the supernatural implications of his art, any reasonable person might acknowledge that Jesus created the longest-lasting movement in the history of the world. Jesus was a top-notch innovator.

But what was the first thing he encountered when he started his grand, three-year creative project? Demons.

The physician Luke writes that Jesus was about thirty years old when he started. He was with his cousin John in the Jordan River when God's Spirit descended from heaven on him. There has been much theological debate about the moment when Jesus takes on an awareness of his divine form. But what are the creative implications of what happened in the river that day? Anyone who has experienced supernatural creativity falling from heaven in complete form, sui generis, can relate to the idea that this moment was the beginning

27

of something great. The movement of Jesus got started the way any great art gets started, with an inspired, fired-up moment.

But, after that awesome day, what is the *very next thing* that happens?

> ***Jesus returned from the Jordan River full of the Holy Spirit, and was led by the Spirit into the wilderness.***

—Luke 4:1

The inspiration gets tested. Vetted. In Jesus' case, tests came in three forms.

The Lie of Lowered Expectations

The lie of lowered expectations is the first demon we encounter in life. It appears somewhere around the fourth grade and trades on the fear that comes before we've ever done anything life-changing with our creative gift. We could call it failure, though this is unfair to failure, because failure, as a representation of unfulfilled past attempts, is a wonderful teacher. What we often describe as failure isn't regret for what has already happened but uncertainty for what happens next. It tells us we stink. It is the false belief that we are not capable of the greatness that burns below our surface, that we can't actually do the dream that we dream. It causes us to grab the first and lowest piece of fruit we see and say, this is good enough. It renders the vast majority of inspiration from heaven stillborn with the simple and seductive temptation of lowered expectations, which becomes self-fulfilling prophecy. It has us believe in a lesser story for ourselves.

This first demon's Turkish delight, or its object of allure, is security. We fear for tomorrow's meal so we accept what the lie gives us, even

28

when our acceptance of it sells out the greatness of the Holy Spirit's descending spark. The lie seems solid and secure. We are led to believe that if we accept this gift, we will allay our fears and satisfy our future.

It works when we are starving artists. It hits us when we are weak. It hit Jesus in his weakness, after a long period of paucity, with the temporal satisfaction of sustenance.

> *The devil said to him, "Since you are God's Son, command this stone to become a loaf of bread."*
>
> —Luke 4:3

As educators have discovered, listening to the lie of lowered expectations results in an increased hesitancy to take risks, a loss of spontaneity, less playfulness, and a general decline in creativity.

The way Jesus defeated this demon was with purpose. Jesus knew, even in the vast open landscape before the whirlwind that was to come, that he had greater passions and purpose and could deal with the short-term trouble of not eating. He dined on the imagination of what was to come.

> *Jesus replied, "It's written, People won't live only by bread."*
>
> —Luke 4:4

The starving artist, the one with only an idea to own, must do the same. Pursuing creativity means we must dine on the imagination of what may come.

This is not a one-off demon, either. It shows up over and over, in every project, even to a seasoned veteran. It appears in every wilderness between initial inspiration and final completion, which is every day that we lose the drive that pushes us to do the thing we're supposed to want to do but somehow don't.

That's why people call it work. The man in the factory that lives vicariously through a professional athlete dreams of the good life and thinks that if he had the life he sees on television, he would be released from his private hell. Meanwhile, the athlete goes through the grind of two-a-day practices, playing with the searing pain of a high ankle sprain, only to lose playing time and get cut, at which point he prays another team will pick him up, even if he has to leave his family on the other side of the country for six months. Both men are trying to get by in the best way they know how, in the world in which they find themselves, listening to the lie that somewhere else, there's a better life than the half-baked one they're living.

Success, or even completion, doesn't banish this demon for good, either. It comes back every time the Spirit descends with new inspiration. When we listen to this demon, we stop making. An adage circulating on the Internet says, "The greatest danger for most of us is not that we aim too high and we miss it, but we aim too low and reach it." Nothing great ever comes from hiding your heart.

The Lie of Self-Glory

Don't think to yourself, my own strength and abilities have produced all this prosperity for me.

—Deuteronomy 8:17

We don't know Samuel Clemens's backstory, but he obviously defeated the first lie. His success is the same as every story of success: through grit and hustle and naiveté and youthful exuberance, we create something new. Our work reaps reward, and for a period we enjoy the treasure of our labor.

But somewhere along the way, our enthusiasm turns into protection, and our focus shifts from making to managing, to protecting what we've made. We lose connection with the source of our passion. Then comes the decline.

This is not just a story of creativity but perhaps *the* story of creativity.

Through the last decade of the old century, the music channel VH1 played this story on a loop in their series *Behind the Music*. Consider the template: a young, talented, hungry rock-and-roll band writes amazing music, works hard, and plays clubs. They get their big break. Clubs become arenas. They experience success, first as joyous wonder, then as a lifestyle to which they become accustomed. They become kings. With arenas come adulation and money and substances, as follies and as metaphors for the broader distractions that keep artists from their art. Under immense pressure to create again but profoundly distracted, the band fractures. Sometimes it occurs in spectacular fashion: people die. Mostly they survive with a permanent loss of the power of their art. A few rise again. The Beatles, Led Zeppelin, Journey, Guns N' Roses, Nirvana—each tell the same story.

This doesn't just happen to rock stars. The same story could be told about every field and endeavor. Scholars work hard and publish fresh ideas; they trudge through airports and conference halls, seeking recognition and acceptance for their ideas; eventually, a big break leads to a job at a good university. Men and women in the business world work insane hours creating new cycles; as the cycle matures, money pours in. Each gets "rich," whatever that means, yet they long to check out of the rat race and take up residence on a beach.

In every case, the things we birth grow and are beautiful, but along the way, our obligations grow, too, and somewhere, we begin to think about maintenance. Our desire to protect takes over. We yearn for earlier days. Our fondness congeals to nostalgia and mythology, and our memories become better than reality. We're not willing to take the same risks we took in the first act of our story. We write it off as something younger people do. We pay for younger teeth and skin when what we really want is to recapture the youthful soul of creative risk.

This is the work of the second demon. It trades on the myth of fame and fortune, that we can all become kings of our own making. It wants us to live solely in the "I rock" side of the Venn diagram of creativity. It wants us to eat the cheese, to believe our own press clippings. It wants us to get final cut because it knows when we stop collaborating, stop listening to others, and genuinely start believing we're the smartest person in the room, that it will have us.

The second demon slyly picks up on the first demon's story line and turns it on its head. After we push the first away, the second comes along and tells us that being a starving artist is the way it was supposed to be, anyway, and that by shooing the first away, we're doing the right thing because the goal is to use our lonely passions to achieve greatness and self-actualization. This demon loves the mythology of Edison and Picasso, the lone genius, the madcap Jackson Pollack in a studio, furiously and with complete self-absorption pumping out private visions, when this is not how the best creativity works.[1] It tells us that we can be kings. It wants us to buy into the lie of self-sufficiency.

Then, if we achieve success, we'll eat the cheese and get snared in the trap that it came from us, it belongs to us, and with it all of the glories therein—all the kingdoms of the world. This insidious demon turns the truth of purpose into the falsehood of self-led purpose:

> *Next the devil led him to a high place and showed him in a single instant all the kingdoms of the world. The devil said, "I will give you this whole domain and the glory of all these kingdoms."*

—Luke 4:5-6

The way Jesus defeated this demon was with proper validation.

> *Jesus answered, "It's written, You will worship the Lord your God and serve only him."*

—Luke 4:8

Jesus knew that, in the flawed human condition, the passion for grand, creative inspiration to change the world easily gets conflated with a sense of self. He knew that it's human to lose our identity in our work and to confuse the inspiration we're given with who we are.

33

The second demon appeals to the desire to be known. We trade in God's glory for our own.

Although he doesn't equate creativity with God's glory, Steven Pressfield concurs that self-glorification is an amateur move. He says that the true creative people must think of themselves as professionals, in the best sense of the word: the one who treats his or her work with utmost respect, who operates with integrity and ethics, who takes responsibility and stays until the job is done. Pressfield notes that the professional doesn't find his or her meaning in the trappings of success:

> As a pro, we may take pride in our work, we may stay late, and come in on weekends, but we recognize that we are not our job descriptions. The amateur, on the other hand, overidentifies with his avocation, his artistic aspiration. . . . Resistance knows that the amateur composer will never write his symphony because he is overly invested in its success and overterrified of its failure.[2]

In spite of the importance of his purpose, Jesus knew not to validate himself by his work, the adulation of others, or the privileges it may bring. He knew that the source of everything he was doing was God. Once he reminded the demon of this truth, the demon disappeared.

Unfortunately, even after banishing these two demons, there is another still to come, and it is the worst.

The Lie of Control

The third demon is as everyday as a corner gas station. It works by legitimizing the corrosive. It seems perfectly natural and right, at one level, to try to control your environment. In fact, many people call it prudence or being wise and protective of your assets. The scientific method is even rooted in the idea of control—isolating variables, testing hypotheses, and verifying data. The spiritual reason Sir Ken Robinson identifies Western thinking as antithetical to creativity is that empiricism eschews the faith that is fundamental to creativity, which in turn is fundamental to life. If we can isolate and verify something, we don't need faith. I am not antiscience, because science can lead to wonder. The achievements of NASA on the moon are an example of science that creates wonder. The problem is the desire, closely associated with scientific thinking, to control our variables and find a definitive answer. Not everything is a nail to the hammer of science.

We lose our creativity not because others take it from us or teach us to think noncreatively. We lose it because we listen to the third demon, who cajoles us into believing that control is the wiser, and even more righteous, choice.

Presumably, the intent behind Mark Twain's publishing company was to control the financial return of his books. As a writer, I love the concept. But it is a fallacy to think we can, or even should try, to control the prosperity of new ideas and creations. When we create, we benefit, and others benefit, too. This is how societies get built. In writing on the early computer industry of the 1970s, Ed Catmull notes that his decision to share his company's work with the world countered the prevailing corporate culture of secrecy. "My view was that we were all so far from achieving our goal that to hoard ideas only impeded our ability to get to this finish line. . . . The benefit of this transparency was not immediately felt, but the relationships and connections we formed, over time, proved far more valuable than we could have imagined."[3]

When we try to restrict and control creativity for the benefit of financial gain, we stifle and sometimes kill it. This is the fundamental problem with copyright. Control is a lie.

This demon even quotes Scripture at us, telling us to seize control of our life (thereby proving it's possible to twist Scripture for selfish gain):

> *The devil brought him into Jerusalem and stood him at the highest point of the temple. He said to him, "Since you are God's Son, throw yourself down from here; for it's written: He will command his angels concerning you, to protect you and they will take you up in their hands so that you won't hit your foot on a stone."*
>
> —Luke 4:9-11

The way Jesus defeated this demon was with surrender.

> *Jesus answered, "It's been said, Don't test the Lord your God."*
>
> —Luke 4:12

Some people go through jobs and friendships and marriages without ever realizing the fundamental problem with control. We engage God for the sake of finding answers when God just wants us to trust. Life is a big mystery, and control is a devilish construct, a straw man that somehow convinces us that the risks of creativity take away from life, when in fact they create life. In the end, when our goal is to hang on to what we've made, we lose the very thing to which we cling. When we replace creativity with control, the result is that we lose life.

Most of the time it seems it's only when we've passed through the fifth level of creative hell that we can emerge into the sunny skies of creative heaven. There's no way to circumvent the demons. Every time, you must confront them. The only way to beat the demon is to stand up to it like a bully on the walk to school. You can't take the next block over forever. That's the fear move. You've got to confront it and say, get behind me. And of course, like with any bully, when you do this, he vanishes. You must learn to stand up to him, not just once but with enough strength that you learn to stand up every day, because tomorrow you're going have to walk down that same sidewalk to school or to work or wherever.

The middle space between inspiration and completion is killer hard, and most of us after a while have had enough and want out. That's perhaps what happened to Mark Twain during *Huck Finn*. Creating amazing work takes a toll.

The corruptive powers of these demons in us, and in those around us who act as a carrier, infect us with blandness, causing us to diminish. They don't take our creativity; to believe this is to assign too much power to the demon. Rather, they cause us willingly to release our creativity.

Starting around fourth grade and appearing again throughout life, we become aware of the power of money and the power of approval. We become fearful of failure and attracted to fame and fortune, at first in small, childlike fashion, and then later in darker, more so-phisticated fashion. For the rest of our lives, our creativity fights an uphill battle with these demons. We summon them in spite of the fact that when they come, they have the power to kill our creativity and damage our soul. We create not to get noticed but because it's in us; yet when we create, we want our work to get noticed. And if what we've created is good, that's usually what happens because others are drawn to those who create and to their work. It, and they, are attractive, and talent brings adulation. Yet, in the resulting praise of the wondrous thing we've made, the demons who first showed up in fourth grade reappear.

And that's what happened to Jesus, too. The end of the story of Je-sus in the wilderness closes with an ominous bit of foreshadowing. "After finishing every temptation, the devil departed from him until the next opportunity" (Luke 4:13).

As long as we have a creative idea, the demons lurk, ready to re-appear. They come again and again throughout life. The demons ap-pear, we listen to them and take credit, and then we lose the wonder of the Creator God who gave us the creativity that began everything. We can't help it; it's the nature of being made in the image of the Creator yet living in, and being marred by, a broken world.

This is the story of creativity, and this is how we lose it. Can we get it back?

5

Leaving Town | The Secret to Rediscovering Creativity

Eyes on the prize, reboot the mission
I've lost the sight, but not the vision.

—The Wallflowers

Leaving Ur

The Abram of Genesis was seventy-five when he had his creative crisis. As the story goes, God told Abram a single word: leave. God didn't tell Abram why or even where he was going. Instead of a plan, he gave Abram a vision: the fulfillment of his long-suffering desire, a family of his own. But this was not just any family; this would be a clan of great proportions. "The LORD said to Abram, 'Leave your land, your family, and your father's household for the land that I will show you. I will make of you a great nation and will bless you. I will make your name respected, and you will be a blessing.'" (Genesis 12:1-2). So Abram left town.

Many of us define ourselves by our life experiences; we think who we are comes from what we've done. We adopt the unexamined idea that our identity is in our history. What is fascinating about Abram is that, at seventy-five, he had already lived a lot of life, and we know none of it. It's not like Abram and his wife were fresh college graduates, looking for new jobs to learn and new lands to conquer. At seventy-five, he had long roots. It's never easy to move to a new land; it's hard enough when you're twenty-two and even harder when you're forty or seventy-five. We have no idea what happened to Abram before God told him to leave town. By leaving town, Abram was making a declaration that his identity was located in someplace other than his history. He wasn't ending; he was beginning.

Perhaps our identity isn't as rooted or fixed as we think. Maybe when we, like Abram, surrender to God, what we did before doesn't have as much to do with what comes next as we might assume.

Judging by the size of his entourage, Abram's trip was a big deal. Yet, in spite of the magnitude of his trip, Abram had no idea where he was going. God had spoken to him in future tense: to a land I will show you. In other words, though God knew what was going on, Abram had no idea what was in store when he left the old place, which makes his leaving all that more remarkable. He didn't wait until he had the new thing lined up before he walked away from the old thing. The physicality of the journey as metaphor breaks down in a digital world; we have no framework to grasp the decision to leave town. He walked away first, without knowing what was to come. From the urge to control, we look for clear signs, but signs don't precede faith; faith precedes signs.

Without a plan or even a known destination, then, Abram had one task: to listen to God. It wasn't Abram's job to make the vision happen, but simply to follow.

Abram took to the road, and though he couldn't have yet known it, his journey would change his identity. When God showed Abram who he was, Abram became someone else. He became a new creation.

The process of getting your creativity back is, in a sense, a process of becoming a new creation. And getting your creativity back may very well mean you have to leave town.

Ditch

Things started out fine for Abram, but after a bit he hit some trouble. In one dicey situation, he leaned on a half-truth—that his wife was his sister—to avoid a possible confrontation with the local ruler, Abimelech. But Abram's attempt to manipulate the situation ended up putting his wife, and others, in danger. (You know you've fouled up when God says to you, "You're as good as dead.") The opposite of righteousness isn't evil; it's distraction. Abram's memory shriveled up. He doubted. He made decisions out of fear. Abram took his eye off the road and went into a ditch.

Yet God protected Abram in spite of his poor listening skills. When Abram gave his wife over to Abimelech, the pagan ruler even called him on his stupidity: "What are you thinking?" Amazingly, Abimelech argues with Abram's God on Abram's behalf. Abram is God's handpicked man, but the foreign king is the one with the moral high ground. Abram, in spite of his poor decision, is blessed. He receives an abundance of wealth from the foreign king, who said, "My land is here available to you." Abram's faith was his defining feature, but he wasn't foolproof. He knew how to drive off the path into a ditch.

But he kept going. Abram didn't just go on a pizza run, either. God sent him on a trip that would take years, even decades, to unfamiliar and sometimes hostile territory. Throughout, God had to keep telling Abram not to be afraid. But in spite of his weakness, God provided for him. That a pagan king got Abram back on the road perhaps says good things about God's faithfulness in our faithlessness. Abram was terrified and screwed up, but he didn't stop moving. This was, literally, Abram's saving grace.

It was Mark Twain's saving grace, as well.

Leaving Connecticut

In spite of his diatribe against the creative process and his myriad business distractions, Mark Twain never fully quit writing.

A year after he finished *Huck Finn*, he began work on *A Connecticut Yankee in King Arthur's Court*, a time-travel satire about a modern man in medieval Europe. Although the book starts with the same light tone as his previous works, it turns dark and apocalyptic by the end—perhaps in some part because its creative gestation paralleled an increasingly difficult and dark personal life. *Connecticut Yankee* came out in 1889; a few years later, unable to keep up with his debt obligations, Clemens filed for bankruptcy, at the age of fifty-nine.

In response, and with apparent great reluctance, Clemens returned to what he knew best. Calling on the success of his Sandwich Islands lectures half a life prior, he left Hartford and embarked on a year-long around-the-world lecture tour. It was taxing; he was no longer a young man. He started in Hawaii and worked his way down through the South Pacific, across the subcontinent, into South Africa, and finally up to England. Along the way he wrote again, and his travelogue became his book *Following the Equator*.

The tour retired his debts but was not without collateral damage. It was on his trip that his daughter died of meningitis. The blow deepened a growing depression that belied a growing international fame. He took to literary criticism, lampooning the work of other novelists and figures. His public, political, and religious opinions sharpened to an uncomfortable edge.

Through diffusion, lifestyle choices, and ultimately personal tragedy, the peak of Samuel Clemens's creative life was over.

Clemens's story is not a moralism that the demons of creativity will appear when things seem the brightest, though this is often true. Rather, the power is in the plot twist that led to his final act. What did he do when he hit his lowest point? Like Abram, Samuel Clemens left town.

What is it about leaving town?

Saddle

Twenty-four years after his first journey, Abram had been given a new name. Now Abraham, he'd learned that identity comes not from your family tree or past decisions but from the new life of faith in God. But again came a test. This test involved his only biological son, Isaac. A sacrifice. I've heard biblical scholars try to soften the horror of this test by establishing context for ancient ritualistic practice. But there is no softening the horror. God asked a man to kill his son, and there's no way Abraham was mute to it.

Yet, early the next morning, he saddled his donkey. Abraham held no conference call or strategic planning session or retreat. With no knowledge of the outcome, he got up early and got on his ride. He trusted, even when it was breaking his heart.

The way to overcome the demons that steal your creativity is to saddle your donkey. Getting on your ride doesn't mean your fear abates or that your heart gets fixed up. It means you do it anyway.

Our preferences skew toward comfort. We want to ride the old thing as long as possible. And while there's nothing wrong with reaping the fruit of a good idea, we have to beware of getting so comfortable that we drive off into a ditch. Leaving town, literally or metaphorically, upsets the status quo and forces risk, which ignites the new thing. New things are dry kindling, the source of the creative spark.

Perhaps there's something you need to be able to walk away from in order to kick God's plan into action. After Abram left, he still lost courage and made some bad decisions. But when we saddle our donkey, we by definition make something new. When we take the risk, we discover it was in us all along.

Dumbo didn't need the feather; the magic was in him.

—Stephen King[1]

Instead of worrying about how God will clean up the mess of our present situation, what if we were to set about the business of co-creating something new? This is the awe of art, no matter what your medium is. Art is a glimpse of the divine, a moment when we are hit with the wonder of truth. To create art of any kind is to engage in wonder making. It is to discover the heart of our Creator God through a cocreative process. The way we confront the demons, the way we get through it, is to go for it more often.

> *Life is ultimately mystery, closely knit to God's creative activity, which didn't stop at creation. God is constantly creating, in us, through us, with us, and to co-create with God is our human calling.*

> —Madeleine L'Engle[2]

Having faith could just as easily be described as having risk because faith is risk, and leaving town is a physical, tangible way of claiming faith. No matter what our type of creative expression, we have within us the ability to make a better future. When we saddle our donkey, we put our faith in God rather than in our ability to control. We allow God to name our identity and position us once again to create.

In Christ, we re-create our God-given identity and lose the destructive impulse. The freeing part is that we realize that we are not responsible for the outcome. Unlike the burden of the third demon's control, when everything is up to us, if we surrender and saddle up, we're free to watch what happens. Outcomes are God's responsibility. Our job is to keep moving and enjoy the view.

I have a prayer that I say on a regular basis. I have come to call it my Creative Prayer, and whenever I remember, I say it again. Here it is:

Use me today, God, and don't let me screw it up.

We're made to be cocreators with God, and it's awesome, awful, and awe-ful. When we create, we take on the character of God, even though we can't handle it, because we're never fully perfected in Christ. Because we're human, whenever we create, we're still vulnerable to temptation. This is why creativity is dangerous business.

And, oddly, God wants it that way—not the brokenness but the lack of control—because if we're smart and don't listen to the demons, we realize that yes, we're not good enough, but God gives us this power anyway; and if we can sidestep the temptation to claim credit and daily surrender our power to God, then perhaps God can use us. And the result is, as Jesus says, even greater things.

What I've learned about faith and what I've learned about creativity is really the same thing. This isn't to say that only those with faith are creative or that those who are creative have faith in God, because often neither is true. People without faith can be creative, and people with faith can be (utterly) uncreative. But to engage in the creative process is to have faith. And it's best to acknowledge the source.

Creativity at its most elemental is life. When we create, we make wonder, to ourselves and to others who benefit from our work. As I eventually discovered, we need to release ourselves and one another to the creative thing that sits idling in the deep places in our souls. If you're a thinker, you can be creative. A humanitarian? An artist? A businessperson? A mom? In each of these worlds and more, we have within us the ability to make a better future by unlocking our creative selves.

But how? By itself, taking a risk isn't necessarily going to lead to creative epiphanies and personal heavens. The risk taking needs to happen in conjunction with a better understanding of the ways or strategies in which we can be creative.

Part Two

The Four Parts of the Creative Life

6

Stardust | The Types of Creative Expression

Junk Filter

My colleague Paul had the purest junk filter of anyone I've ever known.

He quartered no stupidity. He regularly opened the day with a cheery, "It's a beautiful day!" yet could easily take down an innocuous observer's observation on life. A dapper dresser, Paul was quick with a compliment or a snarky comment at another's choice of shirt or shoes. Once he picked a piece of lint off my shoulder and told me I was too nice looking of a person to walk around with fuzz.

Every week in our church-staff creative meeting, Paul sat with coffee in his corner chair, mostly quiet but quick to bellow at someone's gallows humor. When pressed, he would engage in conversations that poked below the surface of church life, such as the relationship of faith and doubt.

Paul believed in brutal honesty. It scared some pastors and churchy folks, but fellow truth tellers among our group valued his insistence on naming much of the play found in church life.

Paul struggled with doubt and perhaps depression. I believe both are related to the fact that the most creative people abhor dissonance and have a hard time living in the suspended chord that is the body of Christ. While many of us can't afford unfiltered honesty, Paul could accept no alternative. As a result, others in the church community pushed against his honest inquiry in ways both appropriate and damaging.

Dishonesty is a subset of ugliness, and ugliness is an affliction to the creative life. Because sin is ugliness, an artist who follows Jesus lives a wounded life, yearning for connection to the wholeness and truth of a Holy God, yet disconnected by darkness within. This potent mixture, this "outrageous humanity," as Pat Conroy wrote, vexes us. We are all saints, and we are all sinners.

Consider the set of "transcendentals" popularized by Plato: Truth, Goodness, and Beauty. These three categories provide us a way of understanding Paul and perhaps ourselves. People who wanted to respond to Paul's art with argument were Truth types. Truth types, on the one hand, seek the resolution of a right answer. They're usually convergent. Artists, on the other hand, are Beauty types. They're comfortable with mystery. They are divergent. Though it would drive Truth types crazy, Paul did not need a final answer to know the truth of something. The church tries to treat the artist's affliction, and the need for honesty is indeed an affliction, with analysis and apologetics.

Some Truth types fear that to acknowledge sin is to condone sin, never recognizing their fear perpetuates sin by creating a cage around Jesus. Beauty types want to explore our humanity and, through it, find a deeper truth than a surface set of facts.

There are also Goodness types, who live between these two poles, usually more concerned with what is loving than what is correct. When Paul and I worked together, our worship team had a healthy mix of all three. One of the great moments that arose from our mix, and there were many, was the Sunday worship during which we hosted Ron Hall and Denver Moore, coauthors of the New York Times best seller *Same Kind of Different As Me*. The book recounts the true story of a wealthy art patron who befriended a homeless man and the changed life each man discovered. That formerly homeless man, Denver Moore, gave a classic call to goodness in our worship service when he said, "Churches in America are full of people studyin'. What we need is less studyin' and more doin'."

The church needs all three. We are built for all three.

Yet the Western church, as the manifestation of the life of faith for followers of Christ, has traditionally served Truth types best, Goodness types second best, and Beauty types the least. For centuries, artists have been finding one another as refugees in a wilderness of analytical thinking. It's easy to retreat behind a screen door of doctrine and moral code. We think we're safe there, protected from profane elements. But of course the screen door not only fails to protect us but also is invisible to those on the outside, who stand in the rain and look with dismissive incredulity through our porous arguments.

Beauty opens the screen door. It invites people in from the rain, but it's dangerous because it exposes us to the elements. We get wet. We are reminded of life, and for many of us, it's painful. Beauty is powerful and threatening. Many in the church fear it.

My friend Paul was regularly crushed by convergent thinkers. He asked too many questions. He was perhaps taught that to find God, he had to move away from his creativity—the very thing to which he was so attuned, the very thing his faith desperately needed.

These are things I would have told Paul if I'd had a chance. Tragically, he passed away before I had a chance to do so. It may not have mattered, but at least I would have had a chance to validate the Beauty in him and help him understand his type of creative expression and its relationship to faith.

Stardust

Every once in a while when I was young, my father would sit down at our upright piano and play "Stardust," or "I Left My Heart in San Francisco." My father is not a pianist and doesn't doodle or play much for fun. Yet he could play these two songs with a melancholy that even today makes my heart ache. I never thought to question how someone who supposedly didn't play the piano could play these two songs so wonderfully. As he played, I sensed a different person, one who I didn't know.

My father also wrote and gave me the affliction of writing. He completed multiple novels and sent them into agents and publishing houses in big manila envelopes with SASEs tucked inside. After he received rejection letters, he put the keyboard away. Later, I asked him about the novels, and he said that he wasn't sure what had happened to them.

He also drew and painted and does still. I don't know if he'd win awards for his work, but my obviously biased eyes like them. I have a couple of his prints hanging in my house. One is an oil of a rusted-out shell of a pickup that he painted when I was young, a rendering of another work he'd seen, as a form of self-teaching. The truck is abandoned in a field and partially obscured by tall grass and a broken fence. Though unable to articulate any reason for it, I liked that painting in my room. Now I look at it and see beauty, rusting in a field, never given wheels to find expression.

Though I've described my father as an artist, he didn't live in a studio. H. Wayne Wilson is retired from his careers as Lieutenant Colonel in the U.S. Army and pastor in The United Methodist Church. In many ways, he is a very different person than Paul. Paul would have probably enjoyed being called a Beauty; I'm not sure my dad takes to the label. But beyond a shared sensibility, they perhaps share another important trait.

My father was never told it was good to be a Beauty. The most important voices in his life told him that to be a good Christian, he had to learn the proper Truth and do the proper Goodness and that creative endeavors were best kept in a separate receptacle called a hobby.

Little Frank: I want to be a musician when I grow up.

Frank's Mother: Honey, you'll have to decide.
You can't do both.

This isn't to say that Dad moped through life. He used, and still uses, his creative gifts as a hobby. He has inspired me. Yet I wonder, how might his career have been different if he'd been freer to apply his creative interests not just to his avocation but to his vocation?

Would he have been able to find stardust not just in a song but in the wonder of everyday creativity?

Transcendental

Each of us has a primary platonic transcendental—Truth, Goodness, and Beauty—and a secondary one, as well. Like my father, I am a Beauty then a Truth. My wife is a Goodness then a Beauty. I am not making these claims from testing, as in an assessment or evaluation, but from intuition. It is just clear to me. Perhaps you intuitively see yourself in this typology as well.

Your transcendental may or may not have anything to do with your vocation. A person can be a lawyer and a Beauty, a musician and a Goodness, or a social worker and a Truth. I know people who fit each of these descriptions. The type is that which defines a person's deepest spiritual and emotional understanding of self, not a hint at what they do. Many times, like those of my father, a person's vocation and primary transcendental can be vastly different.

A person can live a life of complete congruity or total repression of their primary transcendental. Some people never experience, or only briefly experience, an honest connection with their primary transcendental. A person's transcendental is not defined by one's personality type. A person can be strong willed and a Goodness—a justice-minded warrior like U2's Bono—or weak willed and a Truth, or any other combination.

Some might also mistakenly identify someone's primary transcendental based on specific behaviors. Someone might say that I am a Truth person because I like order and a clean desk. But Truth as a transcendental is secondary for me. I don't find myself moved by a clean desk. I am moved by a song or film or piece of writing imbued with deep meaning. I'm merely satisfied by a clean desk.

The goal in any case is congruity or an authentic life or a life of awareness or connection to this primary transcendental trait. But whereas Plato's typology is a good place to begin, it is incomplete. For a fuller exploration of the types of creative expression, a better answer lies with the words of Jesus.

The Four Parts of a Creative Life

God walked through the garden in the cool of the day. This little detail in the creation story, right before Adam and Eve reveal that they ate the apple, is noteworthy, as Genesis isn't known for literary flourish or detail. God didn't just make the world and move on. God stayed a while in it. God made Adam in God's own image, put Adam in the garden, told him to nurture the garden, and gave him the creative responsibility and joy to name all of the animals of the world. He made Eve to accompany Adam. Then God spent time in the garden with them. The Creator pleasured in his creation.

From this first creative act, God made us to be in relationship with, and cocreate with, God. The intimacy of this communion, this creative partnership, is the highest love and the purest existence we can know.

Jesus said, "Love the Lord your God with all your heart and with all your soul and with all your mind and with all your strength."

—Mark 12:29-30 NIV

Later, when Jesus quotes Deuteronomy by saying the greatest commandment is to love the Lord our God with all of our heart, soul, mind, and strength, Jesus is fleshing out the expressions of this love relationship. He is naming the four parts of the creative life, which together describe the action of love and, as God is love, the essence of God. These expressions are more than just behaviors or tactics. They are the essence of who we are as created and creative beings. Loving by heart, mind, soul, and strength is what we're made to do.

Work offers a similar way to understand the presence of these qualities of love, although the word *work* is too loaded and dreary. God's instruction to Adam to name the animals was humankind's first creative project. This happened before the apple. So work isn't part of a life separated from God; it's meant to be a part of a life in communion with God. We're made to participate in the process of creation, to cocreate, and it's a form of work, but joyous work, not drudgery. It's not a 9-to-5 job but the essence of who we are as ones created in the image of the Creator. We're made to express ourselves through heart, mind, soul, and strength, and the expressions we make are how we're to live our lives.

When Jesus reminds us of this relationship, he is naming the sum of experiences that define and give life. These four types of expression are the means by which we as cocreators live with, and love, our Creator. They are the four creative expressions.

In Jesus' simple commandment lies a powerful secret to understanding creativity. These expressions, which closely mirror Plato's transcendental virtues of Truth, Goodness, and Beauty, give us a framework for understanding the creative life. It's no coincidence that in Jesus' description of the greatest thing we can do in life—love—is the secret to unlocking our creative potential. The creativity we seek is nothing more than a connection with our Creator-likeness. When we do as Jesus says the thing that draws us closest to God, we're also at the same time doing the thing that makes us most creative.

Everything we do in a day involves one of these four expressions—our heart, soul, mind, and strength. Passion and zeal are the mark of our heart. Affect and beauty are the mark of our soul. Innovative thinking and new ideas are the mark of our mind. Entrepreneurialism is the mark of our strength.

Every time we do something creative, we use at least one of the four expressions of creativity Jesus identifies—our hearth, mind, soul, and strength—to make meaning and build culture. And when we engage one (or more) of these four, we engage our authentic selves; we're rediscovering our creative genius and in the process becoming a new person.

Therefore, if anyone is in Christ, he is a new creation. The old has passed away; behold, the new has come.

—2 Corinthians 5:17 ESV

Although a developmental goal is to achieve all four, we're gifted and inclined to do one of these things most. Just as we're a Beauty person or a Truth person, each of us gravitates to a specific type of creative expression. One comes most naturally. But each of us is made with the capacity for all four expressions: heart, mind, soul, and strength. After first understanding the story of creativity, then the next task to reclaiming our creative wonder is recapturing these expressions.

But first, there's a counterintuitive trick to looking for creativity. As Jesus says, we have to lose things in order to find them. Instead of running headlong toward every flicker and passion, perhaps we might reflect strategically on our primary creative expression and let a more creative life emerge in our regular work rather than ripple as a distant image on the desert floor. Creativity is not a lightning-bolt experience as much as it is a discipline in the practice of each creative type. Artists paint, draw, and compose; businesspeople make products and services; humanitarians help; scholars think and write—each, in his or her own way, is creative. When we care, feel, solve, and build, we create a more fulfilling future for ourselves and for others. A more creative life begins with understanding the four types. More specifically, it begins with passion.

7

Heart | How to Care Like a Five-Year-Old

Un-Peace

As long as she could remember, Erin Bernhardt wanted to be a Katie Couric–Christiane Amanpour mashup, a sweet and salty combination of a friendly investigative reporter who had the personality of an assertive, well-bred Southern girl.

Focus was never an issue. In middle school, she was a featured reporter for her school's student-led morning announcements. In high school, she edited the yearbook and then produced and hosted a youth-led show on Atlanta's cable public access channel. At the University of Virginia, she co-led a student-run television news program, produced and reported for a local radio station, then landed an internship at the local ABC affiliate, which led to a regional political correspondent role for pundit Larry Sabato. Through talent and the determinism of a long walk in a single direction, Erin was in the process of realizing her childhood dream. But something happened on the way that may reveal the difference between interest and passion.

While in school, Erin developed an interest in the story of Africa. The spark of this interest was more Peter than Paul, a slow story of growth and change tested with time rather than a roadside flash of lightning. Every time she heard a story or saw a news report on Africa, her heart responded. So with graduation came a decision: should she take the job offer for which she'd trained, a career-starting producer and reporter for a local television news station? A lifetime of interest had been preparing her for this moment, and her head told her to do it. But her heart no longer did, for now her heart told her to do something that made no reasonable sense: to become a peace corps volunteer in Madagascar. Her interest had been destabilized by passion, though not destroyed, for passion has a way of co-opting interests and using them for its own purposes.

Madagascar had sparked Erin's passion for a simple reason: it was her source of un-peace. You know how people will talk about having "peace" about a decision? That makes more sense in relief, and I don't mean relief as in the achievement of comfort but the relief when a sculptor lowers the field, leaving the unsculpted parts exposed. Creating relief involves chiseling away the chaff, which is tedious and time consuming. Erin had been chipping away the chaff of her interest over a period of years, and it left a surprising result. Erin's television news job was her career to be, but Africa was her source of discontent.

Wisely, Erin chose Madagascar.

This was Erin's "leaving town" moment, her step away from security toward passion, from money toward love. Passion—not the romantic kind but the motivating kind—is the first prerequisite for any creative act. It is the engine of caring and the fuel for creativity. Creativity and caring are synonymous, both inner caring that means you have passion for something and investment in its outcome, and outer caring where you extend that passion to the lives of other people.

Erin's story is not every person's story. Fortunately for Erin, passion discovered her quickly. As a young, single graduate, she had no golden handcuffs. Not everyone has such luxury. But, almost certainly, in order to pursue your passion, you'll need to leave town in some sense. The passion of your heart will compel you.

Thin Air

The city of Lima, Peru, is both a major city and one of the driest places on earth. Located in a coastal desert region on the edge of the Atacama Desert, Lima receives about a half an inch of rain a year. It has a major water problem. About seven hundred thousand people have no access to clean water for drinking and bathing. Another six hundred thousand rely on cisterns and well water. Whereas it's really dry on the ground in Lima, it's really wet in the air. At an average of more than 90 percent in the summer months, the city's humidity is extraordinarily high.

At Peru's University of Engineering and Technology, enrollment was slumping. Passionate for both their university and the people of their country, administrators needed a way to demonstrate how good engineering can change lives for the better. They approached an ad agency in Chile, and as a means to demonstrate social value in engineering and increase enrollment, the team of engineers and marketers devised a "water billboard."

Using a process of reverse osmosis, they invented a technological trick that converts atmospheric humidity into drinking water. They installed their device on an outdoor billboard in urban Lima. In the first three months after its installation, neighborhood people drew about twenty-five hundred gallons of drinking water from thin air— enough to sustain hundreds of families.

The cost of the technology, about $1,200, was covered by the marketing budget, making it a scalable idea that could help put a dent in the world's clean water problem.

It's a remarkable display of socially conscious advertising and an example of good creativity—creative ideas that offer social value.[1]

Inner Caring

Erin Bernhardt's Africa was a combination of discontent and intrigue, her source of un-peace. Creative Hearts are people who have a deep passion to fix a wrong. They value goodness, a passion for others, and making the world better. You have to feel passionate about something in order to be able to create on it. If that passion is good, if it honors God and loves the world, then it's from God. Goodness is rooted in the character of God; all Goodness comes from God. Goodness is not just a part of God's personality, like an assessment test label, but the summation of God's nature and character.

Give thanks to the LORD because he is good.

—Psalms 107:1

If we do something good, we reflect God, our Creator and the source of our creativity. This is how all creativity, regardless of the proclaimed faith of its maker, reveals God. And how do you know if it's good? If it loves. Because God is love, you take on the character of God—you do good—when you love others. So any creative work that is from God is a good work and loves. I don't mean love in a squishy romantic way, but in a biblical way of sacrificial action, as Jesus' recreative act on the cross reveals God's love for the world. As Jesus instructed, love is the ultimate creative act. In the good it offers, the water billboard reflects God, even if it's not religious.

Now, this sounds quite lofty, to create in order to be good, and our motivations usually don't start in a high place, but in the more immediate place of fulfilling something personal. I don't know anyone who creates out of a burning desire to be "good." I know people who create because they must. Passion doesn't have to be lofty to be honest.

Yet, when our passions are good, like UTEC's water billboard, or when they are the source for something good, like Erin's leaving town moment, they reflect God and take on a greater meaning.

When good, motives that start from self—from inner caring—ultimately become about more than self.

Outer Caring

Erin lasted six months in Madagascar and then spent three weeks in an Atlanta hospital while she recovered from malnutrition from

African parasites. But even though her passion had literally made her sick, she could not let it go. She couldn't un-see problems in Africa.

Her head told her to apply to graduate school so she could pursue work as a communications officer in the United Nations or a non-profit agency. But prayer, which kept her passion strong, pointed her to the hometown television news network, which happened to reach and cover the whole world. As an Atlantan, she realized that through Cable News Network, she could use her interest and experience in news media to tell important stories right away—such as what she'd seen in Africa and the child sex-trafficking market in Atlanta—rather than slowly learn how to do something, as she described, "the official and academic way."

Erin's Peace Corps experience in Madagascar began the fall after her college graduation, so she spent the summer working as an outreach coordinator for an indie rock band, Dispatch, who held a benefit concert at Madison Square Garden in New York City to raise support and awareness for Zimbabwe. Through that event, Erin met the African Children's Choir, which accelerated her passion into a dream, to share their story with the world. This of course never would have happened if she'd taken a "safer" television news reporter position.

Her African Children's Choir dream stayed with her through Madagascar and into her new job at CNN, even as she leveraged her interest in new media into several in-house promotions. After only three years at the network, she became an associate producer for CNN International and shortly after that, on a volunteer trip to Uganda, wrote, shot, and produced a thirty-minute documentary on the choir for CNN International's show *Inside Africa*. The documentary's production and airing was so powerful, it again forced her to leave town. She made the decision to leave the network and produce a full-length documentary on the choir, titled *Imba Means Sing*.

She said, "After it aired, I felt a very significant calling from God to help even more people be positively impacted by their story."[2]

Telling Erin's story in retrospect, like many such stories, cleans it up too much. A replay never captures the original drama. It removes the apprehension and surprise. The replay doesn't reveal how Erin's decade-long experiences were necessary stepping-stones to her creative future. It doesn't reveal how, without a journalism degree or any experience with the hard skills of filmmaking, she needed the time to learn her craft. It doesn't reveal the magnitude of the moment she decided, for the second time, to leave town. Such paths are only clear in the rearview mirror. So how are we supposed to know which way to move?

Pursuit

My life's passion began as an indiscriminate stew of interests in writing, film, computers, and communication, mixed with annoyance at my own lack of understanding of and meaningful connection to church practice. I felt bonded to the church but was intensely bothered by mediocre communication in the church.

Your interests are just that—interests. The secret sauce that mixes your interests with your unique passion is the part that prevents you any comfort. It is your discontent, your anger, even.

I knew little as my passion emerged. Though some called me a tech nut, I was driven not by the technological toys of new media but by my discontent with what I perceived—and still perceive—as the dishonoring and embarrassing way the body of Christ often communicates the gospel of Jesus. As I gained experience, I stumbled around my passions, and along the way, the Holy Spirit moved.

At Gibeon the LORD appeared to Solomon during the night in a dream, and God said, "Ask for whatever you want me to give you." Solomon answered, " . . . I am only a little child and do not know how to carry out my duties. Your servant is here among the people you have chosen, a great people, too numerous to count or number. So give your servant a discerning heart to govern your people and to distinguish between right and wrong."

—1 Kings 3:5-9 NIV

When I was twenty-one, I was inspired by Solomon's prayer for wisdom: I am young and know next to nothing, but I'm here, so give me a discerning mind. I prayed a similar prayer: *Lord, I don't know anything, but if you give me equal mastery of oral, written, and visual communication, I'll use it for the sake of your kingdom.* Much time passed after that. I did little things here and there. I hung out in the production truck of my downtown church's broadcast ministry, even though a church broadcasting its service on television did nothing to reconcile my discontent. Later, I worked as an associate producer for the CBS affiliate's news department in town and then as a youth director at my church. These weren't the answer, either. It seemed like nothing was happening. But really, it was, and I just couldn't see it. I was being formed for a ministry that didn't yet exist.

Passions give birth to enthusiasm, and when we're enthusiastic, we want to push and drive. That ambition can be quite helpful. The ironic part is that when it comes to a "calling," pursuing doesn't work as well as letting go. The counterintuitive trick is to surrender our passion, which comes from God anyway, back to God and then wait. And wait we will because there can be awfully long waits between word and action.

Consider Mary, who was floored by an angel and then left alone for months, with only memories and the occasional sign and wonder to keep her focused on the vision she'd been given. Or Moses, who spent forty years as a shepherd. Or Abram, who left his hometown, only to pass through his destination on the way to a twenty-five-year detour.

The paradox of creativity is that, to the Christ follower, personal fulfillment is a misnomer. A focus on fulfillment belies the truth that when we focus on ourselves, we'll never find ourselves. Our passions exist for a greater purpose than our own fulfillment, yet when we act on a need to do something that gives values to others' lives, fulfillment is what we get in the end anyway.

Maybe you're just beginning the process of preparation that passion produces. Maybe you've been preparing forever, and now something new is happening. Maybe you're already doing one thing you were called to do, and another thing shows up. The beautiful thing is that when the distance between vision and reality finally starts to come together, awesome and unforeseen destinations appear.

After starting a graduate degree in communication, I was led to seminary, to a specialized master's degree in religious communication, as I continued to discern where my passions were leading. It wasn't until I had neared graduation that a unique position opened using new video technology to tell stories at a large church near the seminary I attended. The job merged what four years prior had seemed like a random collection of interests. Within two years I was leading workshops and writing books on technologically savvy storytelling in congregational settings.

Passion starts down low, in the boiler room of dreams and discontent. But the longer we pay attention to it and the more we make decisions based on it, the more it coalesces into something greater: a dedication and a duty to do something not because it makes us feel fulfilled but because we must. Passion pursued eventually becomes a calling. It transcends from a focus on self-fulfillment into something more. It becomes the embodiment of Jesus' commandment to love with all of our heart, which is not self-fulfillment but self-sacrifice.

About her decision to leave CNN, Erin says:

> My friends, family and I prayed a ton about the decision and I
> waited until I had peace in my heart to make it. That's all I had
> though. No funding. No main characters. No perfect crew. No
> signed contract with the choir saying I could do it. It seems a bit
> foolish but I was young and foolish and I am very grateful I was.
> If I knew how hard it would be or how crazy it seemed at the time,
> I might not have trusted my heart enough to leave such a comfort-
> able and "dream" job.[3]

In producing *Imba Means Sing*, Erin realized what it means to live something far greater than an interest or hobby. She discovered a purpose greater than herself. The inner care of her passion has led directly to the outer care of her work for the African Children's Choir.

Our culture's loss of creativity mirrors a loss of zeal, not a thrill-seeking zeal but the kind of passion for which you're willing to take big risks in your life. A creativity that cares is part of how we combat consumption, rediscover our creativity, and help change the world.

Where is your source of discontent? Perhaps you haven't experienced the sort of passionate annoyance that makes you want to change your career path. But, chances are, there is something in your life to which you've thought, *that's wrong,* or *something's missing,* and somebody ought to do something about that, something that seems obvious.

If you have an unrelenting source of un-peace in your life, a discontent that you cannot shake, then perhaps you're experiencing the signals of a Creative Heart and the first seeds of a more creative life. You could numb these thoughts into submission, but what if, instead, you were to make a few decisions based on it and see what happens? Where might a more Creative Heart lead you?

8

Soul | How to Sense Like a Five-Year-Old

Tales of Wonder

Don't be afraid.

As I was preparing for the Christmas season one year in my work as a church's creative director, I realized the frequency with which this phrase kept popping up in Scripture. Every time the angels arrived with news about the impending baby Jesus, they had to include this caveat. The teenage girl, Mary, her betrothed husband-to-be, Joseph, the grimy animal keepers out in fields, the older uncle—each one of them reacted in such a way that prompted the angel to respond with, "Don't be afraid."

I loved that. I called it the "oh no" feeling. Instead of bathing in warm, beatific light, perhaps this is the more honest response we make whenever God shows up.

I built a sermon series around it and called it "Tales of Wonder." It was the Christmas story but told from the point of a view of an artist—one who perceives—rather than a systematic theologian—one who evaluates. Rather than taking the usual approach, I sought to capture some of the sense of presence that each character felt when the angel visited. I wanted to capture the art of the Incarnation rather than the data.

Most theologians are taught to think analytically about the stories of Scripture. They're taught to think about the Scriptures as data or evidence to support an argument or proposition rather than as story. Like anything deeply ingrained, this approach is difficult to recognize. It's like hearing the dialect in our own voice. There's nothing wrong with this approach; analytical thinking can be a form of the Creative Mind. But the difficulty is that when we're taught to judge as with science, we lose the ability to perceive as with art.

Jesus' friends and disciples didn't follow a detached set of principles and propositions. They followed a person. *Kerygma* is the Greek word for the proclamation of the person of Jesus Christ. It is the first calling of the Christian life: to believe in the Messiah with our lives. *Kerygma* is the idea that when we follow Jesus, we change not just our mind but our entire self—our soul. It's much richer and deeper than communicating a "message." As believers, we desire more than cerebral assent to a theology of atonement. We want to know Christ and the power of his suffering.

The deep places in our lives—places of resistance and embrace—are not ultimately reached by instruction.

—Walter Brueggemann[1]

It's about the story of Jesus—not instruction on Jesus—and it's core to a life of Christian faith. The life of faith is as much art as it is analysis. The story is not just a pleasant, ornamental way to absorb teaching and principles. It is the teaching and principles. Narrative, and the art that reveals it, draws us beyond an educated knowing into the knowing of presence, which is a more intimate type of knowing.

The difference between a detached knowing and an intimate knowing is at the heart of what it means to be a Creative Soul. It was what I hoped to communicate in my work that Christmas, and it is critical to recapturing your wonder and creating great things. But it may require you to unlearn something Western society has taught you.

Honesty

In the preface, I described our creations as art, regardless of our vocation or location. We may be engineers or computer geeks or consultants or housewives or academics, but when we create, we become artists, each in our own way.

This isn't a big leap, because for good or for ill, most of us imagine someone artsy when we think of creativity. But the problem is that we often unconsciously think that creativity results in something useful while something that is artsy is merely ornamental. Artistic expression doesn't often quantifiably contribute to the profit and loss statement, yet we know at the same time that creativity can help us answer and invent, discover and build, assist and renew. This almost paradoxical way of thinking about creativity—at once ornamental and utterly necessary for ingenuity and cultural and economic development—runs throughout Western thinking, and it is the biggest problem I see with most advice about creativity. Western culture turns art into artifact, a finished thing we hang on a museum wall.

We live in a pragmatic, utilitarian world in which our "bottom line" questions usually deal with questions of usefulness or profitability.

—Makoto Fujimura[2]

If you wouldn't have even thought to put *bottom line* in quotation marks as artist and author Makoto Fujimura did, or if you wonder why it should be put in quotation marks, then you are a product of a culture that values the scientific method and detached analysis.

Most people advocate a set of tactics to apply for a quick creative fix, but I am not sure that you can draw such bright, clear lines. Creativity is about more than just what is useful in solving a problem. As Victor Hugo wrote: "Madame Magloire had once remarked, with a sort of gentle malice: 'Monseigneur, you who turn everything to account, have, nevertheless, one useless plot. It would be better to grow salads there than bouquets.' 'Madame Magloire,' retorted the Bishop, 'you are mistaken. The beautiful is as useful as the useful.' He added after a pause, 'More so, perhaps.'"[3]

In fact, all art and all creativity is about something much deeper: honesty. Accepting some measure of dishonesty is at the core of what happens when we lose our creativity, and regaining honesty is critical to regaining creativity. People try to capture creativity as a set of practices, but creativity is, at its most fundamental level, simply an ability to speak and live honestly.

Art as ornament inhibits creative thinking because when we make something for purely commercial reasons, we can do it without honesty. Art has myriad definitions, but it is always personal and honest. A five-year-old's creations are always personal. When I say something is art, I mean something is honest, and from the honesty comes beauty.

Every story in this book tells the tale of someone who created something out of personal need. Some have made a fortune; others have not. But each one left town, took a risk, and started something new because he or she had to. Their creative expression came from deep within; it was honest, just as this book is for me.

Understanding the creative act as an artistic act is critical to living a more creative life. To a Creative Soul, creativity isn't just the means by which we solve a problem or make a product. Being creative isn't just writing a blog post or trying a set of tactics at the office. It's much, much deeper than that. Creativity is the means by which we know ourselves. Creative Souls are people with a deep commitment to what is honest. It is who we are. We're meant to make, and this act is personal.

Achieving such awareness is not easy. Ironically, it takes a high level of craft.

Craft

There's an apocryphal story about Clint Eastwood, who, in the 1970s and 1980s, made the transition from critically panned movie star to critically acclaimed director.

The story goes that he had a deal with Warner Brothers, where, for years, he alternated commercial and personal projects. He would create a movie that was green-lighted primarily for the purpose of selling tickets, such as *Heartbreak Ridge*, and then create a deeply personal reflection such as *Bird*, the biopic of saxophonist Charlie Parker, which exercised his love of jazz. He created *The Rookie*, a buddy cop movie with Charlie Sheen, followed by *White Hunter Black Heart*, an exploration of filmmaker John Huston's art. True or not, Eastwood's supposed modus operandi holds promise for creatives as a model. (The miracle is not any supposed alternating deal, but that projects like *Bird* are ever made at all.) Eventually, Eastwood's dating dance of spirit and craft produced a sweet spot of art and commerce: the 1992 film *Unforgiven*. Like Erin Bernhardt's film for CNN International on the African Children's Choir, it was a merger of profession and passion.

Here's the trouble that Eastwood navigated and all Creative Souls must navigate: Creative Souls need honesty, which is personal revelation. Without it, they will never achieve greatness. Yet honesty doesn't always have an audience, because it can be esoteric or unexplained or can unsettle the soul, and what the audience wants is "actionable" solutions to problems and the promise of ease and comfort. It's a paradox.

How do you solve it?

First, the honesty part.

Many of us live with a high degree of unrecognized fear. From fear, we detach, emotionally and intellectually, to protect ourselves. Detachment, of course, is the source of relationship dysfunction, a state of mind that finds comfort in propositions and a search for truth without honesty. Truth and honesty are not the same thing. Someone can be truthful and not be honest. A truthful response is precise but not necessarily honest because it's only concerned with the outcome. When we're detached, we can be truthful and precise, but we may not always be accurate and honest. Honesty is deeper; it's a form of soul alignment that marries intent and spirit with outcome. The creative life—and the spiritual life—is concerned not with truth as extrinsic precision but with honesty as intrinsic motivation.

Creative Souls, regardless of their spiritual state, are highly aware of this distinction. They don't want to engage in something that is fundamentally dishonest, even if technically true. They must "find the truth" in something to engage in it, or they will feel as if they are bastardizing their personhood or selling their birthright for a bowl of soup.

But true creativity can't stop with finding the truth in something.

For a long time, as a creative I screwed up because I never allowed the first part: full, personal expression. I tried to write polished and acceptable out of the gate, and that's impossible to do. You can't do a real first draft with the door open and the apparition of other people in the room, watching. Don't try to interpret your thoughts and feelings inside your head, before you ever put word to the screen or on paper. Instead, just capture what you're thinking and feeling. And don't worry about the beginning, either. Just start making with the current thought that's in your head, even if you have no idea how it relates to what you think you want to eventually say. Start with where you are, and you'll be surprised how it connects with where you want to go. Just make, knowing you have the liberating option of throwing away most everything that comes out.

I write first drafts with the door closed, and second drafts with the door open.

—Stephen King[4]

As a young saxophone student, I worked hard to master my instrument. I listened to the complex riffs of jazz masters Charlie Parker and John Coltrane. I assumed that to be great, I needed to play fast—lots of notes and complexity. I tried to copy the latest David Sanborn solo. I wanted to impress people with my technique. But, in the process, I mostly skipped the essence of the song. One day at school, a trumpet instructor yelled at me in the band hall. I was flying around the keys, and it was likely a bunch of nonsense. I don't recall an emotional connection to what I was doing. Instead of mimicking the speed of a Parker song, I should have searched for the essence of a Parker song. I was precise, but I wasn't honest.

Some people are uncomfortable revealing their own emotions—in music, in conversation, even in prayer. These people, who have also lost their creativity, have unfortunately confused emotional honesty with emotionalism—that to reveal your honest feelings is to be "emotional" or weak, or worse, to manipulate someone. These are incorrect and destructive twists to the truth of honesty. True honesty takes courage and practice.

The best chance Creative Souls have at marrying spirit and connection is through mastery of their craft. This is the second part.

When you create, don't try to visualize the "audience." There is no such large group. We speak of an "audience" in the collective, but in reality they are individuals, with individual preferences and needs and tastes. Don't worry about whether someone will "get it." This takes courage, but if an idea or melody or color speaks to you, put it in. You can always take it out later if it doesn't work, but if you don't put it in, it will be lost. The more you "put it in," the clearer your own style will emerge over time.

At the same time, though, you cannot become lost in your esoteric world. What you do must connect with others.

The advice to create both for yourself and for others seems paradoxical, but it is the paradox where creativity lives. It is the paradox where craft and spirit come together. If you are not connecting with your audience, your work probably lacks either craft or spirit. Perhaps you have seen well-produced, empty-headed films or heard precise, vapid sermons. These are failures of spirit—all the technical skill in the world, and no story to tell. Many say this is Hollywood's problem. However, perhaps you have known—or been— young artists who are blubbering messes of passion, full of spirit, in desperate need of craft to hone a story.

Your craft must exist within the larger creative culture. If you are a designer, your work must have a symbiotic relationship to the basic rules for design, either adhering to them or breaking them. If you are a businessperson, your product must solve a problem that other products introduce but cannot solve. If you're a preacher, your sermon must have some relationship to the principles of homiletics. Craft is essential. Think of craft as the technical aspects of what you do—having the skills and experience to express your visions. There are some who revel in the craft, gearheads who love the process of breathing a story to life. A good filmmaker knows the value of technical proficiency and the need to surround himself or herself with people full of passion for the tools of the trade. But technicians, as valuable as they are, depend on creative vision. They must have the story to tell. This is the spirit.

The spirit is the easy part and yet the most difficult part. It is the act of expressing the source of your inspiration, articulating what moves you and why. Often this only comes through experience. No matter how crude and stumbling, every act of expression, and the response it elicits, is a teacher for improving the means by which we communicate the spirit that moves us.

Creativity starts with a passionate heart. But it needs more than a sense of caring. Creativity requires personal commitment—sweat and tears and maybe blood. A Creative Soul recognizes that when the things we make are honest and personal, yet crafted with skill, that the result is something beautiful.

What activity in your life is deeply personal? What makes you uncomfortable? Perhaps an honest exploration of these recesses may lead to a creative source. If you have a need to create something, not to make a buck but because you need to, perhaps you're experiencing the signals of a Creative Soul and the seeds of a more creative life. You could numb these thoughts into submission, but what if, instead, you were to make a few decisions based on it and see what happens? Where might a more Creative Soul lead you?

9

Mind | How to Think Like a Five-Year-Old

Pendulum

It is not an insignificant detail that Galileo Galilei's father was a professional musician. Vincenzo Galilei was born in Florence in 1525, at the height of the Renaissance. He made his living as a lutenist, composer, theorist, singer, and teacher, and he started a family late. Galileo was the oldest of six children, born when his father was thirty-nine years old. Vincenzo's musical skills attracted powerful European patrons, and Galileo spent his childhood in beautiful homes throughout Europe.

Vincenzo also wrote books on musical theory. While other works on music were theoretical, his combined theory and practice. He was a musical scientist—someone who dared to ask questions about his art.

Since antiquity, the conventional wisdom on strings in music had maintained that a string of a certain length and tension produces a certain tone and that the ratio of string lengths of equal tension producing tones an octave apart is 2:1. Vincenzo questioned this and, with the help of a young adult Galileo, conducted a set of experiments during which he hung and played strings with weights on the bottom. Together, the Galileis discovered that the octave difference is actually 4:1.

I like to think that Galileo was inspired by his father.

Galileo loved mathematics. At the time, mathematics was qualitative and heavily influenced by Aristotelian physics. But Galileo approached this field with a fresh inquisitiveness. For example, Galileo questioned the ancient Greek scientist's understanding that heavier objects fall faster than lighter objects. He wondered about the impact of the environment on falling objects. One day he saw a pendulum swinging in a classroom at his university. If a heavy body's natural place was the center of the universe, as Aristotle taught, why did a pendulum swing perpetually back and forth? There was no explanation. The pendulum became a lifelong obsession and an apt metaphor. His mind, like a pendulum, was in ceaseless motion.

Throughout his life, Galileo created new inventions and made new discoveries. Perhaps his most famous was the telescope, which he invented at the age of forty-five. He had already been interested in the cosmos when he first heard of the invention of a device that would magnify an object three times. After a few months of tinkering, he'd made his own device, which could magnify something twenty times.

The year 1610 was a good one for Galileo and his new tool. The previous fall, he'd observed the behavior of the moon with his new telescope. In January, he discovered Jupiter's four moons. In February, he mapped some constellations. In March, he published his findings. In April, he heard from Johannes Kepler, perhaps the leading expert on astronomy, who thirteen years prior had published *The Cosmographic Mystery*, which argued for the Copernican view of the universe.

A mathematician, physician, lawyer, and church administrator, Copernicus had published his life work the prior century, in the year of his death, 1543. In it he argued that the sun was the center of the universe (the heliocentric view), not the Earth (the geocentric view). Though his work drew from Archimedes and was a clear descendant of both ancient and modern thinking, it was almost universally rejected. His mathematical constructions of the planets were sophisticated, and geocentric proponents used his work to defend their case against him. As with many creative geniuses, his ideas were ahead of their time:

> Thinkers had grown up on the Aristotelian division between the heavens and the earthly region, between perfection and corruption. In Aristotle's physics, bodies moved to their natural places. Stones fell because the natural place of heavy bodies was the center of the universe, and that was why the Earth was there. Accepting Copernicus's system meant abandoning Aristotelian physics. How would birds find their nest again after they had flown from them? Why does a stone thrown up come straight down if the Earth underneath it is rotating rapidly to the east?[1]

Copernicus's work challenged the authority of the church, which interpreted Genesis as geocentric. If Copernicus was right, what did that mean for the church's understanding that the Earth was the center of God's creation?

As with Copernicus, reaction to Galileo's work was controversial in the church. That summer, Galileo accepted a tenured position at the University of Pisa, which came with a side gig as the chief mathematician to the Grand Duke of Tuscany. In December, Galileo recorded Venus's phases. But in January of the next year, oppositional tracts began appearing. The next fall, Galileo took a public position against Aristotle's view of the behavior of bodies in water and repeated it at a state dinner with the powerful Cardinal Maffeo Barberini. Barberini agreed and established a patronage for Galileo to continue his work. But controversy grew. Tommaso Caccini, a Dominican friar, preached a sermon against the Copernican view, in which he accused Galileo of heresy. A colleague of Caccini's filed a letter of complaint to the Inquisition then gave a deposition. Nine months later, Galileo was called to Rome and given a private wrist slap: don't discuss or defend Copernican theory. But while the church published a treatise against Copernican theory, it didn't mention Galileo. The pope privately assured him that he hadn't been on trial or condemned.

Galileo continued his work. Five years later, the pope died, and his successor was none other than former patron Maffeo Barberini, who took the name Pope Urban VIII. In a series of meetings, Urban VIII assured Galileo that he could continue to write about Copernican theory, as long as he treated it as a mathematical hypothesis. Eight years later came Galileo's life work, *Dialogue Concerning the Two Chief World Systems*.

This time, though, the strength of his arguments was too hard to ignore. Galileo's old friend summoned him to Rome. Galileo was ill and susceptible to the raging bubonic plague, and his doctors requested that he stay in Florence. Urban VIII rejected the plea as subterfuge and sent word that if Galileo didn't come voluntarily, he'd come in chains. In Rome, Galileo was found guilty of heresy and ordered under house arrest for the remainder of his life.

Galileo's was a Creative Mind. He could not quit asking really good questions. As such, he was threatening.

> *Galileo's head was on the block*
> *His crime was looking up the truth.*
>
> —Indigo Girls

Shortly before he died, Galileo found rest for the riddle of his life. He figured out how to use a pendulum to power a clock with accuracy.

Like Galileo, some of us are uniquely creative thinkers. Creative Minds are people who refuse to accept the conventional wisdom. They value precision, exactitude, knowledge, the beauty of study, and scholarship in the best sense of the word. Galileo sought answers, not controversy, and because of a stubbornness that never quit asking really good questions, he literally changed the way the world thinks. This is perhaps what Plato meant by the transcendental of Truth. Do we have the capability to do, as Jesus promised, even greater things?

On some level, it is hard to imagine someone like Galileo today. Partly because the power dynamics of church and culture are different, but also because we've deflated big thinking. It seems like all the questions have been answered or at least been dismissed as poor questions. Deconstructionists have taken apart many theories. We're in a postmodern malaise in which we've put aside what came before but don't now know how to move forward. Many are convinced that our future is dependent on a continued search for truth and answers to big questions, but paradoxically they wonder if there's a place for big thinking anymore. The result of all of our deconstruction is that we've lost credibility. In education, theology, and science, we need fresh thinking and the birth of new movements.

What if we could power more creative minds like Galileo's?

Fuel

The annual National Association of Broadcasters conference is gargantuan—a single event with more than one hundred and twenty thousand attendees. It meets every year in Las Vegas because that is the only place in America with enough hotel rooms to house that many people.

I went in 1998 as a young church media director. One of my strongest memories is not a keynote, workshop, or the expo floor (though each was impressive), but the shuttle my team and I took from the hotel the first morning. Over the main entrance to the convention hung a set of massive banners. Each must have been forty feet high—from the roof of the convention center almost to the ground—and were close-up, black-and-white photographs of notable creative figures, such as Alfred Hitchcock, Albert Einstein, and Pablo Picasso. Strategically placed in the negative space of each image were the Apple logo and two words: "Think Different."

Steve Jobs had just reclaimed Apple Computer. At their ebb in 1997, Apple had fallen to 2 percent market share and was losing ground in its last remaining market niche, the film and video production industry. The Think Different campaign was Jobs's trumpet call to his digital diaspora, announcing that Apple wasn't going anywhere. (I wish I'd bought stock after that trip.)

Here is the original, shortened version of the Think Different advertising copy: "Here's to the crazy ones. The rebels. The troublemakers. The ones who see things differently. While some may see them as the crazy ones, we see genius. Because the people who are crazy enough to think they can change the world, are the ones who do."[2]

Apple traded on a countercultural, rebel metaphor. In a world of inhibited creativity, someone who thinks like a five-year-old can seem rebellious. But the campaign was really about something deeper. The campaign's title, Think Different, hints at the shared attribute of its famous set of pitchmen and pitchwomen (one of the featured creatives was Amelia Earhart).

The campaign's effect was both inchoate and dramatic. No one I knew saw the campaign and said, oh, that means Apple is rebranding itself as the company for creative people. They just said, whoa. It was obscure and compelling.

With the benefit of hindsight, Think Different was as subtle as a one-two punch from Muhammad Ali, another one of its featured creatives. To recapture the hearts of its base, Apple appealed to people who wanted to be more creative by naming the way creative people think and, more important, understand their own art. In spite of its poor industry standing, by appealing to people's aspirations, Apple brilliantly resuscitated itself.

Notice how Apple resisted the temptation to explain. Many attempts at creativity fail because we don't let creativity do its work.

We pull up a barstool and rush to the "point," telegraphing a summary and leaving nothing to the imagination.

How do we learn to think differently?

Creativity researchers Land, Torrance, and Robinson each asked the same question, and each concluded that there's something in the way we educate our children that is killing their creativity.

Let's consider the premise that the purpose of education isn't to impart knowledge but to learn how to think. How do schools fare at this often unstated goal? Each researcher agreed that modern schools teach children two kinds of thinking: how to generate ideas and how to evaluate ideas. The first is *divergent* thinking, and the second is *convergent* thinking. Convergent thinking is closed-system analysis; divergent thinking is open-system exploration. Convergent is about finality. Divergent is about possibility. Each uses a different part of the brain.

Convergent (n.): coming closer together

Divergent (n.): tending to develop in different directions

Consider a list of traits:

Convergent Thinking	Divergent Thinking
Evaluation	Imagination
Knowledge	Surprise
Deduction	Provocation
Judgment	Discovery
Criticism	Invention
Assessment	Prediction

90

Of course, to even offer definitions and lists and to evaluate the ways we learn show convergent bias. I included it because we're trained to think of problems with convergence. Convergent thinking is considered problem-solving thinking: you have a problem, and I find a solution. Divergent thinking is nowhere near as ordered.

Some people claim convergent thinking is noncreative and divergent thinking is creative, which makes the two types oppositional. Perhaps, though, they don't compete but are rather complementary, an interdependent yin and yang to the creative process. In a 2007 TED talk, George Land used an apt analogy. Divergent thinking is an accelerator, he said, and convergent thinking is a brake.

The problem for creativity isn't a focus on evaluation or analysis. The problem is that we have learned, and are teaching others, to do both *at the same time*. We write our first drafts as if others are watching. As Land notes, when we teach ourselves and others to make immediate evaluations of ideas, the neurons in our brains literally fight one another. The result is that we diminish the power of our minds. Our need to find an immediate answer takes away the power and potential of many possibilities. When we simultaneously step on the gas and brake pedals, all we do is mess up the engine.

> *Thinking is too closely associated with IQ and deductive reasoning. Before we arrive at the answer, we need to explore more possibilities.*
>
> —Sir Ken Robinson[3]

In my experience, great creative ideas rarely come from a meeting whose sole purpose is to identify and finalize a creative concept. I have wasted a ridiculous amount of time and energy in meetings trying to "be creative." Typically what happens is that my colleagues and I gather to discuss a new project or thematic concept. We suggest a few ideas—"brainstorm"—but quickly get impatient and pounce on the first somewhat decent idea that emerges. We hit the brakes on divergent thinking so we can move on and accomplish the next thing on our list. Many corporations have identified the impatient tendency to try to birth an idea before it has fully gestated and are now moving away from group brainstorming.

Part of the reason that it's so hard to turn on the creative juices in meetings is that we don't start with a blank slate. To best estimate cost, or perhaps out of fear of failure, we usually take a look back at the previous model as a "best practice." By doing this, though, we make an assumption that the vast majority of the new work is going to be a derivative of the old work. Before we even get started, we inhibit ourselves. In our worst-case scenarios, what passes for creativity is not much more than a new veneer on the same product or service. We've learned to evaluate immediately, which hurts our possibilities.

Copernicus, Galileo, and Kepler did not solve an old problem; they asked a new question and in so doing they changed the whole basis on which the old questions had been framed.

—Sir Ken Robinson[4]

Divergent thinking is not a roadside stop on the way to the point. It's an entirely different trip. It is the language of imagination. It invites us to a kind of thinking with which we're unfamiliar, one that opens up a variety of possibilities. And these possibilities offer us a glimpse at a different outcome. To get somewhere, we need to press on the gas a while. We need to test-drive an idea. With planning, I can devote attention to an upcoming project months ahead of its launch. I have time to chew on ideas and develop concepts. I am not suggesting planning a session four months out and then forgetting about it. Instead, we need active, but deadline-free, time to test-drive a concept, then time to allow new ideas to incubate.

In my professional role as a creative director, when I actively consider a metaphor or a concept for a campaign or theme, my senses are heightened to everything I encounter. In the grocery, on the radio, at the house, while engaging my children—the world is full of magnificent raw ore, if I can avoid distraction and stay engaged. This private brainstorming time helps me vet an idea by weighing it against counter concepts. Divergent thinking takes time.

This is perhaps the meaning behind the Internet meme, attributed to Albert Einstein, that "imagination is more important than knowledge." Perhaps this is also why there are so many stories of outsiders and newcomers blowing up an industry. Five-year-old minds see beyond "best practice." They think differently.

One such newcomer was a researcher named James Lovelock.

The Detector

James Lovelock was a young postwar scientist at Britain's prestigious Medical Research Council (MRC) National Institute for Medical Research, located at Mill Hill in London. The National Institute at Mill Hill has long been noted for its scientific achievement. One of its greatest was the invention of the science of gas chromatography, by Archer John Porter Martin, in the 1940s. Gas chromatography is a process that separates a mixture by passing it as a vapor through a medium in which the components move at different rates. Among other things, the separation allows chemists to analyze the purity of a substance. Martin won the Nobel Prize in 1952 for his work, and Mill Hill was, like early NASA, a center of innovation and creativity.

Interestingly, Mill Hill scientists such as Martin were provided ample facilities but no equipment. They were required to invent their own apparatuses for measuring and evaluation. Lovelock says:

> This had a rather interesting consequence. Because we couldn't just buy things off the peg, like they expect to do now, we had to invent. And this meant that, automatically, our equipment was five years in advance of anything on the market, because that's how long it takes a manufacturer to put a new idea into the marketplace, with R&D, production, and so on. So we were ahead of everybody.[5]

Martin's early gas chromatographs could only isolate quantities of samples down to about a milligram. (In biochemistry, single-cell analysis needs to get much more precise, down to the picogram and attogram, which requires a precision accurate to the twelfth power.) As scientists adapted to Martin's new technology, they pushed the envelope. Lovelock was part of a group that devised much more precise devices. His first achievement was the argon detector, which used the rare atmospheric gas argon to help further isolate individual compounds. While developing the argon detector, Lovelock accidentally stumbled onto something greater in 1957—the creation of the Electron Capture Detector (ECD).[6] The ECD could measure a sample down to 100,000 molecules—the most sensitive chemical and analytical device in existence. Lovelock described its power as such: "If somebody spilled a liter bottle of a chemical it could measure in Japan and let it evaporate into the air, you could pick it up [in Great Britain] two weeks later. You could pick it up anywhere in the world with this device in two years—the time it takes to mix with the atmosphere."[7]

The ECD was uniquely sensitive to nasty substances such as pesticides and carcinogens. Using the device, other researchers were able to demonstrate that pesticides such as DDT had spread throughout the global environment. You could find it, as Lovelock said, "in the fat of penguins in Antarctica and the milk of nursing mothers in Finland." The ECD forced the scientific community to acknowledge that pollution was global, not local, as they'd previously assumed. Data from Lovelock's invention enabled Rachel Carson to write *Silent Spring*, which became the basis for the modern environmental movement.

Later, the ECD demonstrated chlorofluorocarbons (CFCs) were building up in concentration, which led to an awareness of the effects of CFCs in the ozone layer. Lovelock's apparatus led to the realization that our planet's climate could be affected by human activity.

Lovelock, like Galileo, asked really good questions. It's worth noting that Lovelock invented the ECD while working in an agenda-free environment. Good science is exploration. The problem now is that much of science is agenda driven, either by virtue of its funding or for the sake of creating direct return for investment. Agenda-driven science seeks specific solutions to meet corporate needs. In such environments, we may be precise, but we're not always accurate.

Early in his career, after having worked in the field professionally, Lovelock was invited to be a professor at Manchester. On a particular test one day, he nailed the experiment so consistently and perfectly that his mentor accused him of cheating. Young scientists at the university just didn't achieve the results he'd achieved. Upon further observation, his mentor realized that Lovelock was indeed a pro. They wondered together: why couldn't the students do it right? Was the university training scientists or just good test takers? Students were precise—technically correct—but not always accurate. Like my saxophone solo of precision but no essence, sometimes their methodologies were sound but results far afield.

A similar incident developed when Lovelock discovered chlorofluorocarbons in the atmosphere with his ECD. Lovelock had been the first to measure them, but American scientists claimed they could measure CFCs with greater accuracy. Results were so varied that eventually the United States National Bureau of Standards did a survey of all labs measuring CFCs. They found the same thing: methodologically correct results that were quite inaccurate. Scientists were confusing precision with accuracy.

In a world of convergence, we may be increasingly precise yet increasingly less accurate. We can name every tree but lose sight of the forest. The paradox of advancing technology is that our increased abilities and focus on precision often get in the way, and when they do, we lose our ability to be creative with our minds.

Sometimes, breakthrough science is not direct and specific but open-ended and exploratory. A Creative Mind knows to be rigid and precise with craft, often the best practitioner in the room, yet at the same time "rebellious" like Apple's campaign, unwilling to engage in groupthink, and independent and assured enough to be ostracized. Are you willing to pursue the idea to its logical end rather than to a predetermined deadline, even if it risks your political standing? Like Galileo, are you willing to live under house arrest? These are the behaviors of a Creative Mind.

There's an epilogue to Lovelock's work on Mill Hill that is a recurring theme of creative geniuses: in spite of his success and an enviable working environment, Lovelock eventually got restless. By the end of the decade, he couldn't continue to perpetuate what he'd built. He needed new problems to explore. But in the small world of professional specialization, he wouldn't do his career any favors by just quitting his enviable post to become an independent researcher. For a while, he didn't know what to do with his life.

His answer came one day in 1961 with an unexpected phone call from Houston, Texas. It seemed an agency had arisen to realize Kennedy's cosmic vision called the National Aeronautics and Space Administration. Executives for NASA were looking for creative scientific minds to help them solve the usually tough question of how to put a man on the moon, and James Lovelock was just the kind of scientist they needed.

What is a question you keep asking yourself, a "what if" question, a curiosity that doesn't accept the conventional wisdom? This kind of thinking may be difficult to find in the recesses of our convergence organized minds, but it is there because we're built for it. Often, "what if" questions aren't world changing. They're just unwilling to accept the regular way of thinking about something and inquisitive about alternate answers.

Rather than bury your crazy thought as impractical, how might you begin to research it for a while and see what happens? Where might a Creative Mind lead you?

10

Strength | How to Build Like
a Five-Year-Old

Compound Problem, Part 1

Cleo McVicker was in a bad place. His company's line of trusty, long-lasting rubbing compound was drying up. Debts were stacking and the economy was floating in the mire at the bottom of a soda fountain barrel. The Great Depression had been brutal on Kutol, the small soap-manufacturing company where McVicker worked as a senior accountant. Kutol had avoided bankruptcy a few years prior, in no small part due to McVicker's creative inventory sell-off. They were making a profit but barely, and their signature product was in decline. They needed something new and big.

The future showed up at Kutol's doorstep one day in the form of Kroger, one of the biggest grocers in the country. The future would have been easy to miss, though, because it was hidden in bad news: Kroger wouldn't be needing as much of their rubbing compound in the future. But, as the conversation turned, they were interested in finding something new—a wallpaper-cleaning product. People were heating their homes with coal-burning fireplaces now, and while it was cheaper than wood, it also made for a nasty house with soot in the air and on the walls, where delicate paper decoration wasn't built to withstand a good scrubbing. Did Kutol have a product that would remove soot from walls without damaging wallpaper?

McVicker and company desperately needed a win. So when Kroger executives asked if they had such a cleaner, they said yes, without hesitation. Kroger executives ordered fifteen thousand cases, with a $5,000 penalty if they didn't deliver on time ($5,000 in the early 1930s is worth almost $100,000 today). The penalty, if applied, would wipe out the company. McVicker and his colleagues signed a contract.

The problem with the deal was that Kutol not only had no such product but also didn't know how to make it. What would they do?

Kutol faced a make-or-break problem.

Hands

Everything has a life span. Change happens; new ideas rise with a new generation, and old ideas fade. This is natural though difficult to weather in a single career or lifetime. For example, most jobs in agrarian societies from two centuries ago no longer exist; in the same way, most of our current industrial jobs are giving way to a digital future.[1]

The peak of the life cycle of a new product or idea is actually short lived. What comes after is what Chris Anderson of *Wired* magazine dubbed the "long tail," or the residual benefit, that goes on forever. One of the biggest challenges to a more creative and fulfilling life is avoiding the atrophy that comes from living in the long tail. Depending on the initial spike, the long tail of a product or service can last years, or even decades. It may take us years to even realize we're in it.

That means that most of us, right now, are riding the long tail. Something creative happened at some point in our life: in our job, our hobby, or a relationship. It was awesome and revolutionary, and it changed not only us but also the world around us, at least a little bit. It created amazing returns in our career, relationships, and finances that continue generating heat today.

But the peak is long past. We're coasting. In life, we spend too much time on the back end of our own creative cycles. We've lost it, but we continue to ride the long tail because it pays the bills. This is the reason 87 percent of us are disillusioned at work and a quarter are so discontent that we are actively trying to sabotage our work.[2] The dissonance has gotten so great that some of us even seek to destroy what's left of our old cycle in a dysfunctional attempt to recover our lost creativity.

If any of this sounds familiar, perhaps the key to your future is a new idea.

The same malaise affects people, organizations, and countries. Polls and common coffeepot conversations tell us to be worried about the state of Western civilization. Are we past the glory days? Everything, people say, is made somewhere else now. Like Kutol, our way of life has rising pressures and waning product lines. We need new thinking and new manufacturing. The old streams just aren't watering anymore.

Don't ask, "How is it that the former days were better than these?" because it isn't wise to ask this.

—Ecclesiastes 7:10

What if, in the middle of such personal and social atrophy, we were to name a future, like Cleo McVicker? What would happen?

Business executives agree on the value of innovation. One study shows that more than 90 percent of executives value company innovation. That's a no-brainer. Yet under half are satisfied with their company's current attempts at innovation. They understand creativity as important but struggle with how to capture it.[3]

Like Cleo McVicker, some of us have Creative Hands. Strength, or the creativity of our hands, is the application of the Creative Heart, Mind, and Soul. It is a creativity of building. When I say building, I don't necessarily mean physical construction, though that may be a part of it. Rather, Creative Hands refers to anything we put together, whether it's a song, a supply chain, a screenplay, an office workflow, or a financial projection.

Some of us are builders. To these people, making something new is one of the easiest and most surefire ways to shake the mundane off. When we make something new, we start the cycle over.

The surprising part of Creative Hands is that it requires the seemingly uncreative work of extensive and careful planning.

Scaffolding

I worked with a Georgia Tech graduate who was our organization's head of operations. He has the mind of an engineer. He is good at naming costs and steps required to complete a project. When some-one on staff sees a glorious vision, he sees scaffolding.

It took me about a year of working with him to figure out that, because I claimed the title Creative Director, he assumed that I'm "artsy" and don't do plans or costs. Sometimes, when discussing a current project, he would ask me if I've considered a specific vari-able. And sometimes I had, but other times, because he is good like this, I hadn't, and I was thankful for his insight. So I didn't get too upset with his bemused tone of voice, because he was adding value to my work. He was right—I don't plan to the extent that he does. Like I said, he's an engineer.

The reality is that most of creativity is actually project manage-ment. Managing resources is a large part of the creative process. But rather than being an inhibitor to creativity, it can be an aid—the creativity of limitation. It's what NASA engineers overcame when they fit a round cartridge in a square hole and what McVicker and the Kutol executives overcame when they made a new core product.

Only a small percentage of my work life is spent in actual free-form creativity. Most of it is spent managing previously initiated creative ideas.

Compound Problem, Part 2

After summoning the chutzpah to make a promise he couldn't yet keep, Cleo McVicker contacted his brother, Noah, an engineer. Cleo asked Noah to go to his lab and experiment with some possibilities. Noah mixed a variety of concoctions together and after several tries produced a working product: a soft, putty-like substance of flour, water, mineral oil, salt, and boric acid. A dirt-distressed house-wife could roll the putty on the walls and pull up the black layer of soot like magic. Noah called Cleo; he had figured it out. Kutol met Kroger's offer. The cleaner was an instant hit and propelled Kutol through the Great Depression, becoming their new signature product.

Cleo McVicker put himself in a difficult position that forced de-livery. The pressure to perform was the basis for his company's most productive work. He seized a remote possibility and said he could do it, even though he had no idea how. Just as with NASA's need for carbon dioxide filters to save the lives of their astronauts, inno-vation emerged from limitation—even desperation. (Perhaps we're most creative when we're ignorant or desperate.)

Kutol Wallpaper Cleaner carried the company for years, but af-ter World War II, it began the inevitable slow fade that every great idea eventually faces. Gas heat was replacing coal heat in American homes. Wallpaper had turned into wall vinyl, and demand for putty cleaner was drying up. Kutol continued to make a small profit on it, but as with all creative inspirations, what was once a booming product had become a long tail of slowly diminishing returns. The Kutol cleaner was reaching the end of its cycle.

Cleo died in a plane crash in 1949, and his nephew Joe took over his job. Kutol carried on. A few years later, during the Christmas season of 1954, Joe's sister-in-law Kay Zufall, a preschool teacher, was looking for something crafty and seasonal for her students. A magazine article suggested making ornaments with Kutol's wall-paper cleaner. The next day, she brought a can to school. The stu-dents, who were four or five years old, loved it. They formed shapes and designs with the putty. Inspired, Kay called her brother-in-law Joe and explained what happened. As she talked, she accidentally pitched an entirely new use for their signature product, one that Kutol would have never thought to explore. Zufall's unsolicited focus group of little creative geniuses had suggested a new product line.

Kutol removed the detergent qualities, gave the material a playful aroma and a bold set of color options, and named their new spinoff product Rainbow Modeling Compound. When she heard the name, Zufall called Joe again, this time with a more directed comment: good product, terrible name. She suggested an alternative: Play-Doh. Kutol had hit the jackpot. Within three years, General Mills bought Play-Doh for $3 million, and fifty years later, it continues to be a worldwide staple of children's playtime.

As part of the 98 percent, many of us assume that brilliant ideas fall down as candy from the heavens to the lucky 2 percent. The reality is that most true innovation does not appear from nowhere but rather lay hidden in plain sight, a variation on what we already know and do, considered from a fresh and different angle. Long before it was ever officially a product of its own, Play-Doh existed as a divergent use of a product designed for an entirely different purpose. Although it may appear that way sometimes, innovation doesn't come from some mystical third heaven. It comes as new variations on existing structures. New ideas might seem random, but they usually have a contextual relationship to what we already know. The first relationship between creativity and strategic planning happens at the idea level. Plans often work best when they're based on derivative ideas, rather than completely new concepts.

Being a creative genius is in part learning to recognize hidden yet visible gems.

Jungle

A bit of backstory: I am writing this book to an outline. While the thoughts in the book are years in gestation, the outline for their construction mostly follows a chapter outline I submitted as a proposal to the book's publisher. I write to this proposal, which forms a map for my thoughts.

The chapter map is my first flyover, an aerial view of the dense undergrowth that I plan on tackling. When my thoughts begin to cross-pollinate into various chapters and create a jungle, as they often do, the way I cut through is to return to this chapter map.

The challenge is when I enter the forest. When I land on a chapter and dive into the growth, I create a second, more detailed map. In this map, I put in every note I've acquired on the topic, whether through late-night flash and scribble, marking from a book I've read, song lyric, or what have you.

Sometimes this acquisition process sorts itself out: in the process of compilation, I see the path I need to take. But sometimes a chapter is a chest high tangle of vine. Precious little of it makes any sense.

When this happens, I get stumped and frustrated. Once in the course of wading through the brush, I got so confused, I just walked away from my computer for about thirty minutes. (When you have a nine-to-five job and four kids, thirty minutes of dedicated writing time is gold. But I was so frustrated, I had to stop.)

When I returned, Elmore Leonard's editing wisdom came to mind: cut out the boring parts. I felt conflicted; most of it was boring, yet I kept fighting the idea that I needed to include it.

That's when I realized what was happening. It was the demon of control working on me. I have been so bound by this lie. To separate what I think I am supposed to say from what I want to say is one of the hardest things I know. Creativity never happens when the lie of control is close. As soon as I name it, it shape-shifts into a false righteousness that tries to convince me that to dismiss its arguments is narcissistic, selfish, and even somehow unchristian. It tries to tell me that it knows best.

So, I closed my entire chapter's worth of notes and created a new page.

Rather than starting with someone else's thoughts, or even my thoughts from a previous day, I considered what mattered right now, in chapter 8 of the book, having just finished chapters 1 through 7 and knowing what needed to happen next. I wrote out a single sentence, looked at it, and decided I liked it as the premise of the chapter. Here is the premise, just as I wrote it: "The power of a creative mind isn't in seeking more precise solutions. It is in asking better questions, like Galileo."

When I created that sentence, what I needed to do next became clear: I should start with a specific anecdote about our tendency to immediately evaluate and how this kills creativity. When I nailed that thought down, I knew I was ready to write the chapter. The whole thing needed to be built on the encouragement to be comfortable withholding evaluation and with the mystery of multiple possibilities.

People desperately seek the lightbulb flash of creative inspiration. But the lightbulb moment is dead without a clear framework, a map to navigate the jungle of thoughts. If you don't plan out your entire project, you're toast.

Steven Pressfield calls this planning process the Foolscap Method. He states that the entire map needs to be able to fit onto one sheet of Foolscap (yellow legal) paper. If you can't map it from beginning to end on one sheet, you don't have it yet.

> *Outline it and block the whole thing in on one page. Do it quick and get it over with. This is, to me, the way professionals work.*

> —Steven Pressfield[4]

Most creativity isn't the romance of a late-night flash or the glamour of a red-carpet release; it's the scaffolding in between, when we see our idea through to its completion. Most of us have had a great idea; creativity is learning to construct the scaffolding it takes to make it happen.

Creativity and project management are not separate realms. Successful creative projects of any kind need a map. Planning is an inexorable part of the creative process. Although my title is Creative Director, some days all I do is project engineering. The inspirations and subsequent big decisions on which projects are based come few and far between. I make maybe a dozen big creative decisions a year and many small ones. Most days, creativity is the grind of seeing a previous inspiration through to a ship date. Creativity needs engineering.

A Creative Heart produces the discontent necessary to make something new, a Creative Soul recognizes that our creativity must be honest and personal, a Creative Mind asks the questions that reorient our thinking, and a Creative Hand crafts the plans that make things happen. Creative Hands is a creativity that builds. It comes not from flashes of light but from a combination of opportunity and carefully constructed plans. It's the application of the un-peace of the heart, the honest affect of the soul and the unconventional thinking of the mind.

Reclaiming the wonder of our created calling means relearning how to love—our work, ourselves, and others, and ultimately God—through these four expressions of the creative life. A strategy for reclaiming wonder, then, begins with exploring these four expressions in your own life.

What is your source of discontentment?
What is deeply personal and possibly
    uncomfortable to consider?
What question or questions do you find
    yourself continually returning to?
What do you enjoy building?

With these creative expressions in mind, now it's time to get to work.

Part Three

How to Become More Creative

11

Blinking Cursor | How to Overcome the Tyranny of Beginning

Knockout

"Let's talk about stifled ambition and broken dreams and people who sit on the curb looking at their dreams go down the drain." Shortly after the box-office success of *Rocky*, young screenwriter-actor-director-producer Sylvester Stallone reflected on his stardust moment.

It was March 24, 1975. Stallone was alone in a movie theater, watching a boxing match between reigning world champion Muhammad Ali and journeyman boxer Chuck Wepner, "The Bayonne Bleeder." To Stallone's surprise, Wepner went the distance, knocking Ali down in the ninth round before finally succumbing to a technical knockout with nineteen seconds left in the fifteenth and final round, when he couldn't get up from Ali's ferocious right.

Wepner was a former marine and barroom bouncer who, prior to the Ali fight, had never had the luxury of full-time training. His ability to maximize the biggest opportunity he'd ever received, to go the distance, spoke to Stallone's own experience:

> If nothing else comes out of that film in the way of awards and accolades, it will still show that an unknown quantity, a totally unmarketable person, can produce a diamond in the rough, a gem. And there are a lot more people like me out there, too, people whose chosen profession denies them opportunity. When that happens, their creative energies begin to swirl around inside, and erode them, and they become envious, vindictive persons who turn to drink. I, myself, turned to fighting.[1]

Prior to *Rocky*, which went on to win three Academy Awards, including Best Picture, on ten nominations, Stallone had only one lead acting credit and no noteworthy writing credits. His creative dreams were withering, but he hung on anyway. Things had gotten so tough he'd had to sell his dog to feed his family. Like his lead character, he needed his own big break.

Stallone let the stardust moment of Wepner's boxing match with Ali marinate for several months, then he channeled his inspiration into a story over the course of a four-day marathon writing session. The result was a screenplay so good he got a six-figure buyout offer, which far surpassed anything he'd ever seen. Yet he'd envisioned himself in the lead role, not a Pacino or a Brando, and refused the offer unless he could play the character of Rocky. Producer Irwin Winkler laughed at him, then raised the offer, and again, and still Stallone held his ground. Finally, he got his wish, by radically reducing the usual upfront advance for a higher percentage of the profits. His gamble worked, as *Rocky*'s box office receipts surpassed $200 million. Stallone became a millionaire.

Improbable? Certainly. Your results, and mine, will vary. But Stallone's rags-to-riches story is not the point. Rather, it was Stallone's relentless need to create and his unwillingness to settle for less, even for food, that is most instructive. Rather than settle for the first demon's temptation of provision in exchange for a lesser story, Stallone clung to his creativity and went the distance, even though it meant that temporarily, he had to dine on his imagination.

Several have studied the habits of famous creative people to look for common denominators. One book of case studies is titled *Breaking In*, which tells how twenty film directors got their start. The stories are disparate, and the basic takeaway is that there are no common denominators, except for one: successful creative people need to create.

The need to create sounds simple, but in fact it's difficult to the point of being crippling and rare enough to celebrate as victory. The blank page's cursor is a tormentor, and the inability to overcome its mocking blinks is one of the primary reasons we never recapture our creativity.

Relentless

A high school English teacher, Julie Aigner-Clark, knew that she wanted her infant daughter, Aspen, to develop an appreciation for the humanities and fine art. A self-described "intense" mom, as many first-time moms are, she wanted to give her baby the best possible head start—particularly when it came to her passion for the liberal arts. Julie read to Aspen. She danced with her. She played classical music for her. She took Aspen to museums in her metro Atlanta region.

But, usually, neither baby nor mom was engaged. The process was difficult, and the work to make it happen was not worth the payoff, to mom or child. More important, Julie realized that going to grown-up or even children's museums wasn't a right fit for her daughter. As a teacher, she knew she needed age-appropriate teaching resources for her home arts classroom. Something baby friendly: "If you're a little baby and you lay in the grass for the first time, the grass is really cool and fascinating to you. If you're an adult, you don't pay any attention to that anymore. My goal was to try to see the world through my baby's eyes and recognize wow, the grass is really green or it feels really interesting."[2]

Julie was thinking like a one-year-old.

She couldn't find what she envisioned anywhere on the market. She thought somebody ought to be doing this. It seemed so obvious. Why not teach infants and young children about their environment and do it in a way that makes sense to them and, oh, while you're at it, expose them to the arts?

One night she had an inspiration that she should just make her own resource. She dismissed it—a ridiculous idea. She had no experience or knowledge in business or product development, nor time, nor desire. She had quit teaching when she was six months pregnant and had no intention of reentering the workforce. She said to herself on multiple occasions, if being a mom was her new job, she was going to be the best she could be.

Several months passed. She continued to search for resources.

None saw the world through the eyes of an infant. In spite of the valid reasons for dismissing her ridiculous idea, Julie's un-peace grew. One night, sufficiently frustrated, she decided to make something.

As a former English teacher, she read books to her daughter all the time. But she wanted to try something with visual and aural stimulation:

> When I have a one-year-old on my lap, what does she want to do? She wants to eat the book. She can't eat the TV screen. So if I sit with her on my lap and I'm watching a great video and it's moving so it's a little more interesting maybe than just looking at a stagnant picture in the book, and we're hearing some great music or some poetry that goes along with it, that's really cool.[3]

She took her husband's video camera to the basement. Even though she had no experience in videography, she wanted to create the video equivalent of a board book, with big images and simple backgrounds. She thought, *I can do simple images.*

The images were indeed simple. Sometimes she used her cat or her own hand playing with a stacking ring toy that her daughter liked. She picked Mozart for the musical score, not because it was what people did—in fact, at the time, no one was talking about classical music for babies—but because it just made sense. Whereas some might see babies as eating and pooping machines, she saw them as little sponges. With her husband's help, she finished the video on her home computer.

Aspen loved it.

In short order, Julie had another inspiration. If her baby loved them so much, would others? She and her husband packaged her homemade video, just as it was. Producing, duplicating, and packaging video in 1996 was no easy task. They spent thousands of dollars on production equipment, pulled from their savings. They shared multiple copies with friends. Eventually, a copy made its way into a trade show, where a retailer of baby products with a small national chain, The Right Start, expressed interest. They negotiated a deal to test market the video with five copies each in six stores. It was her big moment.

A week after the videos hit the sales floor, Julie received a call. All thirty copies had sold in a single day. They needed more.

That first year, Julie made $100,000 on her basement video. It didn't hurt that in that first year, a study called "The Mozart Effect" explored the positive relationship between the development of a child's intelligence and exposure to classical music.[4] Parenting magazine named it "Video of the Year." Five years later, running a small business with eight people, she had grossed over $20 million.

But the money was merely concomitant. The revenue was wonderful, but I think her original motives weren't actually about money. I think she was simply compelled to make something cool for her daughter. Her motives were intrinsic, which is what drives creativity most of the time anyway. (It is a mistake to try to motivate a creative person using money or other extrinsic factors. Although money is always important, it can't outlast inspiration.) If Julie had wondered how she could make a million dollars, I doubt she would have figured out a way to do that. Instead, she began with creativity: an original idea. A desire to have fun and make stuff, like my five-year-old's definition of creativity. A desire to solve a problem for her daughter. A source of un-peace.

Early on, Julie sat down at her kitchen table with her daughter's crayons and drew a little head modeled after Albert Einstein. When Disney bought her out five years later, they kept her logo, and to this day, when Julie sees a Disney Baby Einstein product with her crayoned picture on front, she is reminded of her inspiration, and a frustration that changed her life and the lives of many other people.

As the book on aspiring filmmakers instructs, this is the one common denominator: creative people just need to create. There are no rules, no insider secrets or cheat sequence to get you where you want to go. To rediscover your creativity, you need to just begin making stuff. Your creative calling is a path you must carve yourself. Don't say, "I want to be a writer," or, "I want to make large automobiles," or, "I want to solve the mystery of fusion power." No one is going to bestow that title on you. Film studios don't send recruiters to film schools. Publishing houses don't troll English departments, and HGTV won't ring your bell for tips on your fabulous garden plan. In creativity, there are no wannabes. You either do it, or you don't.

Instead, say, "I am a maker of large automobiles," and then start making them. Say, "I am a writer," and then start writing. Just go to the basement or the garage, and start making something. Craft models. Do experiments. Initially you will make a lot of bad art. But as you continue, you will do it better, and eventually you will discover a niche. People will begin to notice. It will develop in time, as it should. Keep success stories like that of Julie in front of you as sources of hope but not as instruction manuals. Every story is different. You must make your own. And the only way to get there is by creating, for a regular and sustained period of time.

If your plan requires getting picked, and you're not getting picked, you need a new plan.

—Seth Godin[5]

Creating is real work, and there are no short cuts. This is true for famous creatives, and it's true for the rest of us. It sounds easy in theory, but in reality, especially if you're trying to rediscover a latent creativity, it will scare you to death.

Old Master

A fellow creative professional told me that she hated the tormenting cursor on a blank screen and much preferred to mark up a first draft. She is what David Galenson calls an "experimental innovator," or an Old Master.[6] This is one of the two creative types. Unfortunately, being an Old Master is the hard way.

Old Masters improve slowly through long dedication to their craft. Clint Eastwood's filmography in the back quarter of his life is by far the best. Robert Frost wrote 92 percent of his poems after the age of forty. Beethoven didn't compose the Ninth Symphony until he was fully deaf; he didn't need to hear, because by then, his dedication had led to complete internalization.

To Galenson, painter Paul Cézanne is the archetype of the Old Master, an arduous maker who worked out his creative vision not through beatific light beaming from his brush but through sweat, anguish, and endless revision. Malcolm Gladwell notes abut Cézanne, "He would paint a scene, then repaint it, then paint it again. He was notorious for slashing his canvases to pieces in fits of frustration."[7]

Old Masters learn slowly, agonizingly. They often have teachers and mentors. In fact, they're the reason that teachers teach, while their counterparts, Young Geniuses, for the most part, don't need such aid. Young Geniuses are prodigies. Galenson calls this type of creative person a "conceptual innovator." They don't understand conventional thinking. They're compelled to do what seems natural to them, even if it's radical to others. They are swift and decisive in acting on their unique vision. Picasso, Galenson's archetype of the Young Genius, created *Les Demoiselles d'Avignon*, which many consider the most important painting of the twentieth century, when he was twenty-six. Einstein published his first theory of relativity at twenty-six. Orson Welles made *Citizen Kane* at twenty-six. Maya Lin made the Vietnam War Memorial at twenty-three. Mozart composed *The Marriage of Figaro* at thirty.

Young Geniuses do revolutionary work early in life, but here's the catch: they rarely repeat it. It is as if some creative people are dispatched to our culture from the great beyond with a specific new variety of beauty, which, once earthed, no longer needs its carrier. The success of *To Kill a Mockingbird* appeared to overwhelm a young Harper Lee. Ezra Pound produced 85 percent of his poems before the age of forty. Picasso and Einstein lived long lives but likewise did not repeat their early achievements.

Conceptual innovators have no trouble beginning. They hold a complete mental image of their work prior to beginning and in fact find it difficult to work without a solid understanding of where they're going. They aren't big on drafts, edits, and revisions; their work emerges primarily in a single output. The creative process is simply execution. Consider Sylvester Stallone: a young man writes a screenplay in one marathon sitting and never regenerates the accolades given to his earliest work.

Galenson's labels are both helpful and limiting, as labels tend to be. They imply that the conceptual innovator is gifted and the experimental innovator merely works hard. Neither is exclusive, and sometimes the opposite applies. The labels play into the wrong conventional wisdom that the world is neatly divided into creatives and noncreatives, or conversely, the labels play into a false dichotomy that if you're creative, you're one or the other.

I did an informal poll with some designer and artist colleagues and friends. Every single one of them identified with the Old Master rather than the Young Genius. Certainly this is in part due to humility and to the fear that somehow we have a creative expiration date. But beyond that, I think it reveals something deeper, that we mythologize creativity as the work of the gifted few, when, for the vast majority, creativity isn't romantic but a sustained and sometimes grueling discipline. Most of us need editing.

Gladwell makes the observation that while we might think of Old Masters as undiscovered gems or late starters, which assumes that the Young Genius and Old Master are basically the same but with different market experiences, the real difference is that Old Masters "simply aren't much good until late in their careers."[8] They become masters through, to reference another Gladwell axiom, applying themselves to their craft for at least ten thousand hours.

In other words, perhaps a few of us receive creative inspiration gift-wrapped from heaven, but what Galenson calls the Old Master is in fact the creative process by which the vast majority of us function. Most of us discover greatness not by fully formed manifestation but by laying brick. You show me a romantic story of someone hitting it big, and I'll show you someone who worked in obscurity for years, if not decades.

In the creative process, most of us have no idea what will emerge when we begin and can even partway feel like we have achieved, and will achieve, nothing. In every good thing I've created, there's been at least one place where I thought what I was doing was going to fail. Inevitably, I have to go through the "I Stink" phase.

Further, most Old Masters have a hard time discerning the end of the work and will continue to tinker even after publication.

Creativity needs room to explore. Most of us don't enjoy being monitored while we work; we'd rather retreat and spend time with an idea before emerging for feedback and revisions. We might feel or come across as less confident or assured in our creativity than Young Geniuses because of the nature of our creative process. We need space to find our best work. You have to work at it, and the more you work at it, the better you will get. Experimentation is how the creative process works. This means we have to allocate sufficient gestation time. We need to set expectations for our creativity. Your pursuit of a more creative life will actually make your life more difficult, not easier, at least in the short term. As Paul Graham notes,

> If you asked random people on the street if they'd like to be able to draw like Leonardo, you'd find most would say something like 'Oh, I can't draw.' This is more a statement of intention than fact; it means, I'm not going to try. Because the fact is, if you took a random person off the street and somehow got them to work as hard as they possibly could at drawing for the next twenty years,

they'd get surprisingly far. But it would require a great moral effort; it would mean staring failure in the eye every day for years.[9]

In other words, the prospect of such real work is sufficient to keep
most people in their post-fourth-grade stupor.

I don't want to kid you. Being creative is hard, mentally and phys-
ically, and more importantly psychologically. Making something
new, by definition, forces change. We must abandon the comfort
of what came before. The most mature version of our old mediocre
experience can look pretty good compared to the raw, painful birth
of our new creative idea. Embracing creativity requires willingness
for you to change yourself.

Perhaps this sounds pie in the sky, a mythology that serves Hollywood but isn't actionable in the real world. You may find comfort in
knowing that there's really only one thing you have to do.

The One Thing You Have to Do

I'd been at my first job, producing videos and creative elements
for worship at a large church, for several years. It was the late
1990s, and my colleagues and I were some of the first to do what
was becoming a national trend. Other church leaders were asking
questions. We felt a passion to help them. I was frustrated at the
limitations in my ability to do so from the position I held. So when a
nonprofit company that had close ties to our church's denomination
wooed me and a friend and colleague on staff, we took the bait.

Our patron company was known for printing the denomination's
newspapers. They wanted to start a "digital division," and they had
cash reserves from the 150-year-old long tail of their original cre-

ative inspiration. We couldn't believe the resources at our disposal. For a brief period, we thought we were "living the dream."

Shortly after arriving, though, it became painfully clear that our definition of a digital division and their definition of a digital division did not align. Compounded by the presence of many voices, and our own youthful exuberance and ineptitude, the situation soon became untenable. After eighteen months of increasing tension, we resigned, independently but within a few hours of each other. We both left town.

I went home that night pretty freaked out. Since we'd started, I had added a five-month-old daughter and a mortgage to my list of responsibilities. Life had gotten a lot more complicated. I talked to my wife about the prospect of starting a company with my friend and his wife and doing the same thing that we had been doing but on our own. We all got together for dinner to brainstorm a plan. I was scared; I said that I could see this happening someday, but we were not ready yet. I was not ready yet. We had no seed money, except for a single speaking engagement the next month.

The next day, we got an email from our ex-employer. They wanted to continue the relationship contractually but said we'd first need to establish ourselves as a separate company. I think their intention was to hold us to a business relationship that they perhaps weren't sure we could meet. What we got from them, though, was a major contract that became the foundation on which we built our venture. Their stipulation forced us to move forward when we otherwise might not have.

The choice to resign precipitated the shingle-hanging. The end came before the beginning. This is God's way. Faith precedes signs, not the other way around. Action comes first.

A little boy ran up to a high fence, took off his hat and threw it over. "Why did you do that?" a man nearby asked. "I need to get to the other side and I thought if I threw my hat over there I would try real hard to get over the fence."

—Leonard Sweet[10]

Now, I don't necessarily recommend quitting your job without a plan B, and I offer my story not with glory, because I was forced to do what I lacked the courage to do on my own. But part of beginning is taking a first, large, scary step into an abyss of waiting. Not a little step, but a significant one. This is the one thing you have to do. It is the test. You don't get to lie on the couch until the doorbell rings and you greet a delivery guy holding your Oscar. You have to take a step, and it will come to you, a little at a time. And the first step will probably stink. And several after that will, too. That's okay—it's part of the process. This is a way in which creativity and faith are kindred spirits. Faith is a prerequisite to a recovered creativity. In fact, it is best to assume up front that God will never send you to someplace awesome. That's your job.

I like to think of myself as an Old Master. My best work is yet to come, and every day that I make something new, I am climbing toward this foggy summit. I stumble along and slowly figure things out. And the way I do this is through discipline to the raw ore of creative inspiration. So, the hardest thing is to take a big step. The next question is how.

12

Minecraft | How to Find a
Workable Creative Process

My children love a video game called Minecraft. I downloaded it at one point on my phone, tried to navigate the 1980s Atari-like graphics, and deleted it. Later, after three of my four children saved up and purchased matching iPad Minis, they discovered it. It has become their obsession. Now, when they finish homework, they log on together and let the digital avatars talk to one another.

As far as video games go, there are worse games over which they could obsess. It's a "sandbox" game, which means their blocky selves can wander freely in an open digital world, doing stuff and talking with other blocky people. They also fight bad guys like large spiders and zombies, but the fun of the game is in building things. I assumed they build homes, but the other day my son Christian told me he has a friend who built a working lawnmower. My younger daughter Joslyn proudly showed off her library. My older daughter Kaylyn added, "One time I built a church, but my sister let loose a bunch of chickens in my church, and I got really mad at her, and we had to kill all the chickens." Minecraft is digerati Legos.

It's also massively popular. It was first published as a full release version in late 2011 and quickly received several awards for design, innovation, and playability. In its first two years, it sold over thirty-three million copies across a variety of platforms. The programmer who designed Minecraft is Markus Persson. He lives in Sweden and goes by the online name "Notch." He started programming on his father's Commodore 128 computer as a seven-year-old. Programming on a Commodore 128 is like cycling the Tour de France on a Big Wheel.

Clearly, Notch thinks like a five-year-old. He can make mining compelling. It's not like mines are new. The oldest known mine, at forty-three thousand years old, is the Lion Cave in Swaziland, and the earliest miners were flint finders. Finding flint led to the creation of the first tools, which in turn were used to discover better minerals and to make better tools. Egypt became the first dominant civilization in the world because they discovered the full resources of a mine, including building materials, pigments, and currency such as gold and silver. Basically, mining is as old as dirt and the source of all human development. It's also boring. Who would've thought that a game about mining would be a hit?

But then again, isn't that what creativity is all about? The ideas that unlock our creative future lay about us. We just don't see them. They seem typical and even boring. Creative gold is hidden right below our feet.

Discovering is, as Notch Persson knows, a mining process.

The Gifted and the Grinder

One of the enduring pieces of advice from my father is that creative success comes not from the inspiration of a whimsical muse but from the hospital-cornered-bedsheet discipline of a creative routine. A grind.

I've tried to take his advice to heart. In writing this book, I have on many mornings risen early to grab thirty minutes of writing time before the daily routine begins. At one time, this routine was at night, before bed. I have tried both ends of the day. Neither work. I'm a fairly disciplined guy, yet I have struggled with this advice my whole life.

Steven Pressfield says to get over it. He says, just show up and work, and the muse will obey. I suppose this is good advice for the majority of people, who were not raised by the military, who could use a routine kick in the pants. But routine has never been a problem for me, and yet ordered creative time is inconsistently productive at best.

No matter how I structure my time, I have never found a routine that matches the muse's schedule. Instead, creative inspiration seems to show up at horribly inconvenient times, like in the middle of a meeting or while driving home in my truck. It seems some days I can write, and other days I can only choke, spit, and gag.

After a while I began to recognize a pattern. Inspiration is more likely to come when (a) my mind is in fifth gear, not first or second; and (b) when I am around the scenery of other human interaction, which builds associations and connections, both pleasant and annoying. (This faux interaction may be why so many people like coffeehouses for creating.) In other words, the muse likes experience.

Although good creative things can happen in private at home, better things tend to happen when the world is bumping up against us.

Yes, routine is important. But if I am a slave to a grind, my routine may yield nothing. Yes, inspiration is important, but if I wait around for inspiration during my routine, I'll grow spiderwebs creating boring stuff nobody should be forced to read. Dad and Pressfield say to write daily and that it's a discipline; and there's truth to this, but you cannot deny the power of the muse and the ability to do more in one hour with inspiration than days of mining without a discovery.

According to one major-league baseball front office executive, there are two types of athletes in pro sports—the "talent," or the naturally gifted athlete, and the "grinder," the one who makes it through grit and determination. It's easy to label people with categories such as creative genius or creative dunce, talent or grit. Perhaps, though, these assumptions are facile. The reality is somewhere in between. How do you incorporate both the muse and the grind into a single creative process?

Sometimes creativity is finding a vein of pure gold. Sometimes it's the backbreaking labor of turning ore into usable ingots. The mining metaphor is the answer to the question about the gift versus the grinder.

How does this work? The process begins with prospecting, or exploring to find raw ore. With discovery comes evaluation: what is the enrichment factor? Not every idea is financially feasible or marketable. If the idea is great, then it's time to set up an exploration program, a proposal, or business plan, and start extracting. The plan is very important because it helps define what's necessary and what's extraneous. With the plan in place you can begin to go mining, and refining, which is the interrelated process of finding new ideas and refining them into useable thoughts. Although these are separate steps I don't mean to imply that they're always clean and distinct. The catch is to think of them as different steps. Once the mining and refining are done, compile and ship.

Let's look at each step in more detail.

A Creative Process

My undergraduate university campus has a quad area with sidewalks in squares around big lawns. For years on dry days, students ignored the sidewalks and cut across the lawn in diagonal swaths between buildings. Over time, unsightly grooves developed in the big green squares. The groundskeepers fought in vain, with signs and regular reseeding efforts. One fall when I returned to campus, I discovered they'd given up and finally turned the grooves into cement sidewalks.

The creative process doesn't always fit into prescribed recommendations from others who would beautify our landscapes. You've got to do what works for you.

A working habit he has had from the beginning, Hemingway stands when he writes. He stands in a pair of his oversized loafers on the worn skin of a lesser kudu—the typewriter and the reading board chest-high opposite him.

—George Plimpton[1]

Every creative person has some degree of indigenous work habits—peculiar maybe, to the outsider, but natural to the creative person, fitting temperament and personal need. Veteran creative people, and honest ones, embrace their own eccentricities. They know what it takes to create. For example, I have a short attention span and am prone to dismissing boring things at a biochemical level. I drift away and even fall asleep. Ask my mom, who put up with me sleeping through church on more than one occasion. Or my wife. I used to be embarrassed about this trait. I have come to recognize it as a cue that something isn't working. If it is something over which I have no control, such as when hearing a sermon, I use the opportunity to analyze why it isn't working and create a list of things that I would do to fix it. If it's something that is part of my responsibility, such as a book I am writing, my boredom and disengagement are personal cues to make it better.

Another habit is to listen to movie soundtracks while I read and write. I like the sweeping epic kind, such as *The Lord of the Rings* or *Legends of the Fall* or *Braveheart*. The music flavors the writing with possibility. It doesn't always happen, but sometimes the soundtrack sends me from an awareness of the computer screen into a time-bending idea excursion. It is during these sessions I often find my best morsels.

All this to say that creativity is personal. Next, I outline a seven-step process that works for me. Your process may be very different, and part of the joy of plunging into the creative life is discovering what your creative process is.

First: Prospecting

Consumption gets a bit of a bad rap. Every story needs a story-teller and a story receiver. The problem with the Internet is that the world is now full of talkers and no listeners. Everyone's busy building "platform." A storytelling culture needs both story receivers, or consumers, and storytellers, or creators. It's our pleasure as consumers to be moved, thrilled, and changed. I'm pro-creator, but I'm not anticonsumer. After all, it's the stories we consume that inspire us to create.

Creativity starts with input. The bummer is that to be a creator, you must be willing to ruin your favorite moments.

In the late 1990s, I was editing short films for work at a rapid clip, about one a week. At the time, editing was heavily influenced by MTV, a quick cut style with moving cameras that created a faux-cinema-verité-on-steroids look, with early motion graphics thrown in for spice. Some bad imitations were literally nauseating, but a few movies, such as the first *Bourne* movie, nailed it.

After watching one such sequence I decided it was time to learn it, so I imported a film sequence into my computer's video-editing software and watched it frame by frame, forward and backward, until I'd figured out what the filmmakers had done.

This experience taught me a key component of creativity: I needed to be able to sacrifice my inspirations at the altar of learning. Let yourself experience it, but then go back and detach yourself emotionally from it, in order to figure out why it moved you so. This is how you learn.

Creativity begins with exploration and initial mining, to find a vein of valuable raw ore and then identify its depth and value. Pay careful attention to your interests. What consistently intrigues, moves, and even bothers you? Intrigue occurs when you want to learn more about something. Moved is when you're emotionally altered by it.

Both are necessary. The subject you keep returning to, again and again, is the first sign that you might want to put your creative energy on it and make a project out of it. Perhaps you love home remodeling shows and interior design. Maybe you should explore what it would take to become a realtor, with a special interest in helping people find older gems and redoing them.

Second: Feasibility

How do you determine if an idea is valid? First, research the market: is there a clear need?

Understanding consumer needs is one of the biggest stumbling blocks to creativity that works. While working as a leadership acquisitions editor at a publishing house, I consulted a large-church pastor on a book he was writing about transitions in leadership. The topic is perpetually timely, as upwards of one hundred thousand congregations change pastors in a given year in America. I suggested a number of subtitles with an application hook, such as *Ten Things Every New Pastor Should Do*. The author rejected each one. He didn't like what he perceived to be a reductionist approach to a theological topic. I understood the pushback against a purely tactical approach—every creator wants to think of what they're doing as deep and meaningful, instead of an instructional manual. The pastor wanted to tell his story, and as he described it, "let the reader draw conclusions."

Creators tend to think in terms of features—what their new idea does. Consumers think in terms of benefit—what's in it for me? Any new creation worth pursuing needs tangible benefit. I told the large-church pastor that he needed to draw the conclusions for the reader. The project must solve the problem. Otherwise, it's a swirling dervish, a wild cloud of exotic thoughts that never hits the ground of application. (Read the majority of blog posts ever written.) The large-church pastor was focused on the big ideas of his role as a creator, which is good, but could not see the topic from the needs of the consumer, which is bad.

You can be creative all day long, but if you want to have an effect on others—and make a living—your idea must provide a clear benefit.

Third: Planning

All creativity has passion. Creativity that ships has a plan.

After Samuel Clemens's death, his survivors found several distinct manuscripts and writings containing similar characters and themes in various states of composition. Their creation had covered the last ten years of his life. His biographer, Albert Bigelow Payne, patched four of them, an introductory work, and three substantially composed but unfinished versions of the story into a single novel entitled *The Mysterious Stranger* and published it in 1916, eight years after Clemens died.

Unfinished creative works are common. Sometimes death or finances are the cause; other times, perhaps including Clemens's story, the cause is emotional trauma and the damage of the demons of creativity. Often, an overly ambitious plan, a bad plan, or the inability to adhere to a plan derails the project.

A plan is a proposal, a blueprint, a scope of work agreement. It's crucial at this stage to both build a plan and stick to it, because creativity grows like a flowerbed vine, and if you don't prune it, it will choke out your big idea and you will never ship. Even in the year that this book grew from exploration to finished manuscript, I dealt with many new creative ideas that, while intriguing, threatened to derail the project. I had to be merciless about saving this new raw ore for later use.

Fourth: Mining

At one time, one of my favorite diversions was the television show *Chuck*, a pop-culture dramedy about a geeky accidental spy who gets the girl. Chuck became a spy by inadvertently looking at a sequence of classified images transmitted from his old college buddy, a real spy. The sequence of images uploaded a comprehensive database of spy knowledge into Chuck's head. At crucial times in the narrative, Chuck would "flash." His eyes would roll back in his head, and he would download a relevant set of data into his memory cache, such as how to do kung fu just before the bad guy brought the pain.

I love the flash metaphor. It is what happens to me when I sit up in bed at three in the morning with the compulsive need to write down an idea. This late-night need has been a problem for years. My wife is used to my overnight adventures. She'll ask, "Are you okay?" while I hop up, searching for my glasses and a pen to preserve my unfettered vision on an envelope or a ridiculously long string of sticky notes.

> *Over the years I have come to recognize that the work often knows more than I do.*
>
> —Madeleine L'Engle[2]

This is the essence of revelation, of God permitting a glimpse of the Divine Self. It is a gift. If you've ever had a sudden rush of an idea or read a book or sat in a dark theater and had a thrilling moment of hyper-real wow when you feel you've been given a glimpse into an alternate universe of hidden truth, then thank God. It is the beginning of vision.

When I was younger, I sometimes confused discontent with anger, a righteous indignation at perceived and real slights to the way things ought to be. I'd think, somebody ought to do something about this. Indignation served me well, too. Much of my first two books were written that way. But to call it anger is to mischaracterize it. The flash is actually a gift, a revelation of insight at a crucial time.

We cannot always control when the moment of revelation appears. It may be when you finally have quiet and opportunity for reflection, after the kids are in bed and your phone has let you be. It may be in the middle of a hectic moment but triggered by a memory or an action. The only thing we can control is the ability to recognize the idea and develop the practice of capturing it before it blows away.

I spoke to a friend who has written dozens of books and asked him how he organizes his thoughts. He laughed and pulled out a pile of ripped paper from his coat pocket. To most people it could easily be mistaken for trash. But they were his thoughts and ideas, captured on the fly, yet to be translated into a larger theme.

Learning to capture these thoughts as they happen is one of the greatest and most important insights of the 2 percent. Almost all of us have creative thoughts throughout the day. A mom thinks of a new way to finally track coupons well. An operations executive realizes the person he should call to solve a recurring workflow problem. Our screwup is that these thoughts fire off like meteors in our mind in the middle of a sunny day, and they are easily missed. They'll shoot by our consciousness, and we miss them altogether, or we'll think to ourselves, *I need to write that down*, which is a famous last word.

So grab the flashes. And as the flashes come, resist the urge to edit. This I believe is the single hardest part of the creative process. We want to trim, cut, and delete before it is time to do so. Instead, what you need is a free-flowing, open-ended period of input. You need new material to work with! This is when divergent thinking is important. Most of us in the 98 percent are comfortable with editing and trimming and deleting—judging work, our own and that of others. But we're not as comfortable with making new work. We'd rather refine than mine. It is the making of new work that is courageous. It is one thing to refine, but another altogether to mine the ore.

If you don't know yourself well, you may not be harnessing this gift. At various times, I have let mine waste. It is our job to learn to recognize it as a gift and to capture it. You must get used to recognizing the idea and capturing it as soon as it happens, no matter what you're doing.

Don't just give this lip service. Most of us can refine. But the vast majority of us have little to no experience in mining, and we're scared to death of it. If you want to create, you must get good at capturing the ideas when they come. And come they will. Occasionally you will hit a mother lode vein of an idea. In my experience, it's not always clean division; sometimes raw ore comes in a flash and sometimes in the grind.

Sometimes, it takes a lot of mining before you hit a vein. That's why it's important to have an uninterrupted period. It wasn't until four solid pages of writing about mines (horrid material) that I hit the vein that resulted in the opening anecdote for this chapter. That's over one thousand words, most of which I ended up cutting.

Having said this, here's a warning to the opposite extreme. It's easy to get lost in a cave and never return to the surface. Some do this and as a result never actually finish anything, which is just as bad as not having a plan to begin with.

Fifth: Refining

Anyone who's ever been on a factory floor or by a potter's wheel or in a maternity room understands that making something new is messy and chaotic, exhilarating and exhausting. Although creativity and control are mostly frenemies, and control is not a helpmate to faith, I have discovered a surprising truth. Creativity and control are not opposites. Rather, there are stages to the creative process.

Steel doesn't come straight from raw ore, you know. The raw material must first be formed into intermediate building blocks, which are called ingots, or materials cast into shapes suitable for further processing. Refining turns the ore of a late-night inspiration into a polished ingot. A creative mother lode means nothing without extracting and refining.

When you're busily mining and after a while you look up and you don't have any fresh ore bodies or veins to work with, then the better solution is not to continue to mess around in the dirt with nothing to show for it but to spend your time processing what you've already found. Most of my regularly scheduled creative time isn't raw mining but the refining of previous ideas into ingots.

When in doubt, tidy up.

—Brian Eno[3]

Depending on the nature and location of the ore body, more waste than ore can be recovered during the life of a mine. I'll sometimes capture ideas that don't have an immediate use. When I was younger, I'd try to include everything in the current project, and the result was sometimes incomprehensible. Now I am more disciplined about sticking to the plan and storing extra material away for later. You've got to be selective. But be careful not to throw "waste" away. Rather than hit delete, put unused ideas in a separate bin for later.

Sixth: Repeat

The same process—mining and refining—goes on over and over.

I initially worked for ninety minutes the day I wrote the first draft for this chapter. Feeling empty, I stepped away to address the log of messages that had accumulated from my wife, four kids, extended family, and my job. Later that day, I returned for round two.

When stuck, don't press, but get up and move around and do something else and talk to someone and clean the house or whatever. As I'm doing those things, I spot more veins, so I come back and work them some more. When I've totally worked the ground dry, then I move my energy to processing and cleaning up and making the ingots, which in my case are the chapters that later form the entire book. I work on sections of a project at a time. For each section I alternately mine, process, and make ingots. (A tip: having a blog has helped me tremendously, as the limitation of a six-hundred- to eight-hundred-word deadline to introduce a salient idea and move toward action forces me to tighten my focus.)

As these pieces fit in place, I begin to see the final product.

Seventh: Compilation

Also known as polishing. This is the most satisfying stage, at least to me. When I bring all of the pieces together I am finally able to see it as a single entity and can make adjustments and emphasize overarching themes. The result of this tedious process, when done right, is creativity that ships and satisfaction that follows.

But this doesn't mean you've got it figured out, because while creativity gives life, it can also kill you.

13

Half-Life | Why We Must Constantly Keep Creating

Chapters

One of the surprising things I learned while in publishing was the one-year business plan. For some reason I'd assumed that books had a longer projected life span than one year. But like anything else, publishing operates on business cycles. An idea becomes a product or a service. Shortly after it ships, it peaks and then begins a long descent. The idea doesn't die immediately but lives on for years in the long tail.

The head of any product is what happens in the first period, which in publishing is the first year, and the tail is what happens after. The long tail works in the aggregate: when grouped together, many products all living out the end of their life span make a sustainable source of revenue.

Cleo McVicker, the accountant at Kutol, made a living on a wallpaper cleaner product whose long tail lasted for decades. Its brilliant successor idea, Play-Doh, has had a long tail going for sixty years. That's a creative triumph.

The problem is that not every creative idea has that strong of a tail. We hope they do. If we've fallen in love with our idea, then of course we don't want it to end, so we hang on. It's been good to us. And of course there's nothing wrong with squeezing every penny out of a good idea. But what sometimes happens is that we hang on to our old idea perhaps longer than we should.

Here's the danger of creative success: creativity has a half-life. In fact, it's best to assume that everything you do in life moves you one step forward. One step only. After that, it's useless. Our work is always vulnerable to the what-have-you-done-lately phenomenon. Sometimes, a sustained relationship or previous accomplishment will bear fruit, like a perky perennial that pops up in a future garden. But we can't build a crop on the past. We have to continue to seed a new garden, every year. Because the danger is that, once we grow something good, we get stuck. We don't see the future coming. We wake up one day and find our achievements wilted.

Consider: an entrepreneur stumbles on an amazingly successful product and on its back constructs an international business. But over the succeeding few years, the market shifts, and suddenly she is forced to lay off hundreds of employees, a full 25 percent of her workforce. While her head was down, operating the machine she'd built, her king-making product bled out.

Or consider education: most of us spend four years of our life in high school, crunching homework assignments and positioning ourselves for good SAT scores, all for a single transaction into a university. After that, our high school numbers—not the knowledge, but our creative input—are useless. Then, we do the same thing in college and gain another diploma, the vast majority of which are ultimately unused.

We create a body of work. We use it. We move on.

I don't mean to suggest that what we do becomes worthless. The residual value of our work—the knowledge and wisdom we acquire—builds. Depending on our choices, our creative work can last a lifetime. There is great value, and personal joy, in the body of work we accumulate. But its half-life is much shorter.

Think of your creations as chapters in a story. As scenes in a plot that advances, we live chapters that move us to other chapters. Sometimes the scenery changes drastically, and what we once made no longer matters. The plot of our life builds even as old chapters become irrelevant to the current story line.

I had been a young gun in the church leadership world and a first-to-market author on a trending subject. At the half-baked age of twenty-six, I was leading seminars and keynotes on the creative use of screens in worship services. I thought I had arrived. Over time, this thought took to my creative lining as a sickness. I became comfortable in the world my work had birthed. I extended it as long as I could, perhaps past its half-life as a creative work. Because what happened was that many more people came along and put a twist on what I had done. Some became first to market on social media; others on the antiscreen movement. One day, I woke up and realized that innovation lad left the station without me. I realized that perhaps I couldn't ride my big idea for an entire career. I still liked it and still today like it, but I'd realized that perhaps it was on the back end of its life cycle.

The temptation to ride the long tail too long is the work of our old friends, the anticreative demons. We seize control and ride the tail as long as we can. And while there's nothing wrong with reaping the fruit of a good idea, if that's all we do, we end up in a ditch. The trick is to start the next new idea before the old idea dies.

As it turns out, there's a formula for avoiding the half-life problem.

The Sigmoid Curve

First developed by Charles Handy, the Sigmoid Curve charts the dilemma of when to begin new product cycles.[1] Bret Simmons explains:

> Things start slow in the beginning. For a while it may even seem like we made a bad decision or started down the wrong path. Then at point A, things start to take off. From point A to point B is a period of accelerating growth and performance. But at point B, we begin to experience the asymptotic limits to growth. And by point C, we experience the pain of inevitable decline. If we wait until point C or even point B to realize that what we are doing will no longer work, we face tremendous hardship and competitive peril.[2]

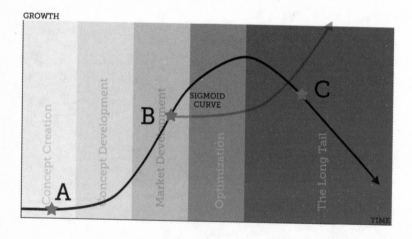

The trick is never to reach C but to start a new growth curve at point B. The problem, of course, is that point B is precisely when you're reaping the reward of point A. This is counterintuitive because it doesn't seem to make any sense to launch a new thing when the existing thing is going gangbusters:

> However, to be truly successful is . . . to jump off the current curve when it is nearing its peak and start on the bottom of another curve. This can be very hard to do, because just as you are reaping the rewards of your work and application, you find yourself at the bottom of another learning curve. This entails more pain, since growth always involves pain to some degree. It doesn't appear to make sense to change just as you are doing so well. There is even, perhaps, a sense of loss—why throw away something which is mature and bringing a reward for something untested and new?[3]

Sustained creativity requires us constantly to begin anew. If we wait until the previous peak has passed, it's too late. We're going to decline. Exactly when we should expect to reap the rewards of our work, we need to be hard at work, creating the next thing. Creative geniuses know the irony: when we are truly creative, we find success, and once we find success, the temptation is to protect. Often without realizing it, we turn from love to money, and before we know it, we've hit C and will face an inevitable decline before the next thing can begin to rise. In other words, we must be careful to never give up making new wonder, because the 98 percent try to extend a good thing way past its expiration date.

Don't allow yourself to rest on the laurels of success. Look forward. Start over. Keep making. Five-year-olds understand that the answer is just to have fun and make stuff. Regardless of what you do, or how you do it, the secret is to keep creating.

Fast Balls

Mike Fast is a baseball nut. He has been since he was a child rooting for the Kansas City Royals from his Oklahoma panhandle farmhouse. He has always loved numbers, and baseball is the perfect sport for a numbers-loving boy. It is both science and theater.

When he graduated from Oklahoma University with an electrical engineering/physics degree, he took a job in Austin, Texas, doing failure analysis. It paid well, and he enjoyed the detailed numbers work for a while. Eventually, though, his interest and career opportunities began to fade. At some point, the rope on every budding career gets taut, and the only thing past the frayed end is more of the same or a thicker rope tied to rearranging money and people.

Mike knew himself well enough to know that he wouldn't do well rearranging money and people. Like many people in their thirties and forties, he was stuck. Some people call it a mid-life crisis, but it's really a creative crisis. He was making a good living, but he no longer enjoyed it, and his prospects for career advancement were low. What was to come next?

Mike found himself drifting back to his boyhood hobby. Watching baseball didn't pay the bills, but he enjoyed it; and now in his thirties, he brought a different eye to the game. He began to watch pitchers more closely. He started tracking pitches and developed a system to analyze their success ratios. After a while, he shared his hobby with a friend. The extensive research shined. His friend was blown away by the quality of the work and suggested that Mike start a blog.

To be good you've gotta have a lot of little boy in you.

—Roy Campanella[4]

The domain name was easy: fastballs.wordpress.com. He posted his first entry, a mammoth file with dozens of links, and got a few comments, including one person who requested proper credit. Mike learned blog etiquette and began posting several analysis and links entries a month, including complicated graphs such as the various locations of curveballs and sliders to left-handed and right-handed hitters. He started to get some feedback. He developed fans.

He explored what it would take to turn his hobby into a business, but that was difficult to visualize, and with kids to support, he saw no way to unchain the golden handcuffs of his miserable, well-paid job. So, he continued to focus on research and his blog.

A few years passed. In his continued research, he honed in on specific players. One day he got an e-mail asking for some more analysis. It was from a major-league pitcher.

Stunned, Mike agreed. For a while, the pitcher's golden e-mail seemed isolated, but with time a strange phenomenon began occurring. His Sigmoid A began to turn into a B. His Twitter-follower count climbed into the thousands. He began to do paid articles for sabermetrics publications and websites.

Then, the Pittsburgh Pirates e-mailed.

It was just an inquiry, of course, but they wanted to explore the possibility of Mike doing some work with their club. Mike wasn't sure if the opportunity was a real job, though, and hesitated. By now he had a following, and a small side income. Was this real? Besides, he was settled in Texas, with a wife, two toddlers, and twins on the way. A move to Pennsylvania seemed highly risky.

He agonized through weeks of messages.

Then, a curveball: perhaps as a result of his established engineer's salary or the new crop of hard-working twentysomethings without families to support or the fact that he wasn't fully engaged in his work—really, that he hated it—he was laid off. Now, he had to make a move. Risk had been thrust on him.

Should he pursue the Pirates? Was it even really a job? Things were coming to a head, and fast. He had less than sixty days to start a new life.

Then, the Tampa Bay Rays wrote. Then, the St. Louis Cardinals. He received an invitation to Major League Baseball's Winter Meetings. He was going to go hang out with the pros! It was a dream scenario, but there was still the nagging problem of location. He and his wife didn't feel at peace with an interstate move. Finally, on the last day of the meetings, he learned about one more interested club: the in-state Houston Astros.

The negotiations were brief. He had to take a pay cut to lose the golden handcuffs and become a big-time Major League Baseball analyst. And a three-hour move was necessary—relatively small sacrifices, as it turned out, to pursue a more fulfilling life.

Four months later, Mike was on the home page of ESPN's Grantland website, discussing the Astros' front office rebuilding effort.

The Story of Creativity

Mike Fast's story is a story of creativity. As with Erin Bernhardt's story, telling Mike's story in retrospect cleans it up too much. Mike is my brother-in-law; I watched his story unfold in real time, and it wasn't clean. It was frightening and nerve wracking and at the same time full of life.

Each one of us has such a story in us. We have within us a supernatural power to create, and pursuing it may lead to amazing things. But in most of us, the story is latent. We've lost sight of it, and as a result, we spend huge swaths of our life hanging on to the shards of a once beautiful dream, thinking that the existing, long-tail remnant to which we cling is better than the promise of a new image.

The Sigmoid Curve is a scientific explanation of a spiritual truth. To avoid succumbing to the demons of creativity, we must constantly, over and over again, step out in faith. For a while, A dreams can be soaring B achievements, but eventually every idea becomes a fading C tail. The creative challenge is to celebrate our old ideas but not cling to them and instead continually push back to a new A. This is how we avoid the half-life of brokenness and creative decline.

So how do we set off from the existing thing, whether a shiny, upward B, or a fading long tail?

If you've been through the fourth-grade slump and don't feel creative, or if you've succumbed to the demons of failure, fame, or fortune and you are at a wall, then the way to fix it is to leave town. To make something new. No one loves the process of becoming, though. It's painful. We want to be finished, with our job hassles, our health ailment, our interminable schooling, or our debt. We think we want the comfort of consumption, but consumption leads to death. We find life in the uncontrolled thrill of creating something new.

The reality is that whether we're being creative or not, we're not in control. We only have two options in life: to be conformed or to be transformed. Our only choice is the choice between allowing the patterns of an uncreative world to shape us or allowing an exhilarating Creator God to shape us. Notice the passive voice in each. In neither are we in charge.

> *Don't be conformed to the patterns of this world, but be transformed by the renewing of your minds so that you can figure out what God's will is—what is good and pleasing and mature.*

> —Romans 12:2

To be conformed is what happens when we do nothing. It is easy to stay on the couch of our dreams, watching others create while being conformed into a consumer. This is the default choice for many.

To be transformed is the harder choice. When we renew our minds—and hearts and souls and hands—the new things we create creates a new us, inside and out. Eventually, as we do this over and over, we realize that we're changed, our identity is changed, and we've somehow become more like Christ. Creativity is a process of faith formation; it is a means by which God transforms us. This is what the redeeming work of the creative life does to us and for us.

In theological terms, healing our uncreative tendencies is called sanctification—the process of making holy, or whole. Creativity is intrinsically tied to this need for wholeness. The more we move toward a sense of wholeness or sanctification, then the more creativity we experience. Faith leads to creativity, and creativity leads to faith. This is why creativity and faith are kindred spirits.

The good news is that while creativity is about you working, it's also about God working in you. When you're being transforming into the likeness of Christ, you're actually making a new life. The move toward God is a move toward change and a new life. Leaving town means getting to work—not necessarily at doing things but at the spiritual work of re-creation.

Like faith, creativity is the assurance of a hoped-for finished work. Until we are made complete, being creative, which is an act of cocreation with our Creator God, is as good as it gets. The act of creating, of surrender and faith—expressed as love of heart, mind, soul, and strength toward God—draws us into the intimacy of cocreation and is as close in this life as we'll ever get to the heart of God.

Faith isn't a passive wailing but an act of growth and a commitment to the future. So is creativity. When we create, we are actively working for tomorrow. We are making something new and fulfilling our own best hopes. Creativity is the active ingredient of faith. Faith is the catalyst that converts dreams to plans.

To create is to gain a glimpse of what God does. Creativity redeems. It heals. We take what was damaged and make something new, like shards of glass made beautiful by their arrangement into pieces of stained glass and being illuminated by the light of Christ. When you create something, you're acting in God's image and, in the process, becoming more like God made flesh. You're becoming more of a little Christ. And in the process, you're making for your-self a better and more fulfilling future.

True creativity is an act of God because it is done not for money but because it's honest, a love act of heart, mind, soul, and strength. Whenever we solve, care, express, or build, and we do it from an honest place, we are expressing our deepest and truest self and drawing closer to the One who created us. When you make a big de-cision like Mike Fast or Erin Bernhardt because you're compelled to do what your heart calls, you're acting as God designed you to act—to create, as the One from whom you were created.

The way to rediscover our creativity is to keep climbing, keep moving forward, past the demons that tell us we're no good and the demons that tell us we rock, past the promise of lesser stories and the vanity of glory, past the need to control, to a place of surrender and work and a place of new beginnings. When we discover that the sustaining power of this journey is Christ, then we are on our way to reclaiming the wonder of a more creative and fulfilling life.

A Few Creative Suggestions

Ten Ways to Find Good Ideas

Creativity is all around us. Five-year-old minds have radar for good ideas—where they are and how to spot them. Here are ten ways to find good ideas.

1. Good ideas appear on their own schedule

Good ideas rarely come in a business meeting whose purpose is to generate good ideas. Sometimes, they appear as part of a disciplined creative routine. Just as often, they eschew creative routine altogether.

2. Good ideas appear when you're doing something else

If ideas don't appear at business meetings, then when and where do they appear? They come not in offices or other sterile environments to me but in relaxing settings such as when I am with friends, reading, or watching a good program. The keyword is *Input*. You can't do creative work living on the fumes of an old idea. Good ideas require fresh input. If your work environment is stressful, then you will struggle to generate good ideas.

3. Good ideas appear after hours

Creative people, or people who are adept at finding good ideas, are rarely "off."

"Off" is a false construct used to cajole people into doing work for which they are not created. If you are working according to your passions, you may find that ideas come with little correlation to punching the time clock. This is why many people who think like five-year-olds seem nonlinear and scatterbrained. They're not flaky; their radar is just incessantly pinging for brilliance.

4. Good ideas don't appear near tasks

I actually schedule "creative time" on my calendar by protecting two to three blocks each week (each block is usually three hours) from meetings and appointments. But, even if you can escape other people's questions, it is still an act of will to avoid the task list.

Often my best time for good ideas is the afternoon commute home. I am tired but firing on all cylinders. With a half hour in the car and my phone on silent, my mind sometimes escapes the tyranny of the task list to diverge onto obscure paths, where undiscovered gems lay peeking through the brush.

5. Good ideas don't appear with noisy fanfare

"Noisy fanfare" is writer Steven Pressfield's phrase. He uses the metaphor for time spent observing an Idaho potato farm assembly line, where thousands of potatoes rolled by on a conveyor belt every hour. In the midst of the dogs is an occasional perfect potato.

There's no flag in it or beatific light shining down. It's just there amid the regulars and the rottens. It's your job to spot it.

6. You've got to teach yourself to spot a good idea

Some claim that good ideas have a feel to them. I agree in theory, but the difficulty is learning the feeling. It's taken me years. Like the assembly-line worker who spots the good potatoes, practice is essential. It's taken me years to recognize it, and I am still learning. Here are five things I look for when separating a good idea from a mediocre idea.

Good ideas tap into the human condition

The human condition is intrinsic, like hating Mondays and male pattern baldness or loving windfalls and when someone flirts with you. Psychologists and marketers have identified a few basic human needs such as belonging, love, identity, autonomy, hope, authenticity, and significance. You can do worse than comparing your idea to people's basic needs.

Though it sounds obsequious, always vet your idea from the audience's point of view: what's in it for me? That is the question they're asking, and you should, too.

Good ideas are exact

Good ideas start with specific concepts, not vague generalities. They provide tangible solutions to both emotional and market needs. An emotional need is the gut feeling, often fear, that drives your audience, such as the human conditions above. A market need is a problem that needs to be addressed. What problem does the idea solve?

159

Good ideas create common ground

Eventually, everyone gets beaten down by a bad boss or notices their neck sagging. Some life experiences are just universal. Others are common enough to base assumptions on, such as the fear of taking home a new baby for the first time or the thrill of going to an opening night. Good ideas touch something that connects with a life most live. How does yours create common ground with the reader?

Good ideas are indigenous

I helped a Japanese American church leader on his book to improve the leadership skills of the leaders in his care. His material read like a dissertation. The concepts were solid but typical. One key concept repeatedly surfaced in the material: leadership can be improved. As I read it, I remembered the word *kaizen*, a post–World War II corporate concept that many credit with the resurrection of Japan. It is a compound word: the first symbol, 改, *kai*, means "to change, to correct;" the second symbol, 善, *zen*, means "good."

Together, kaizen roughly means "continuous correction and improvement." I suggested a new title: *Spiritual Kaizen: How to Become a Better Church Leader*. We used Japanese symbols to create striking images that helped the leaders remember the key message.

Good ideas embody their purpose

A ministry wanted to raise awareness and further fund global mission partnerships to aid causes such as improved secondary education and an end to human trafficking. As the church leader talked about the partnerships, he spoke of spiritual connection with others around the world. As he described the relationships, he interlocked his fingers. His words and gestures led me to an image of fabric woven together. We collaborated, and the idea grew into a successful campaign that both illustrated and added to the ministry's goals.

Every idea exists for a purpose—whether to sell a product or service or to make the world a better place. Good ones don't sit on top of the purpose like icing, perhaps tasty but superfluous. They embody the purpose, adding meaning and vibrancy. Can you look at an idea with no annotations and deduce the core to which it points?

7. You'll doubt yourself as soon as you get the feeling

We're trained to self-inhibit; we don't know what it's like to explore an idea, because as soon as we find a halfway decent one, we conjure up criticisms from phantoms.

To avoid self-flagellation, we immediately polish our raw ore into a finished product. Since, to paraphrase Hemingway, all first drafts are feces, this is like polishing a piece of excrement.

Resist the polishing temptation. When the feeling appears, stay in the room a while.

8. You'll think the good idea looks used

One of the biggest reasons good ideas go by unnoticed is that they don't look all that new or different. They can feel like they've been done before. But don't let it fool you. This sense of familiarity is not a negative. It is in fact a sign that it's a good idea. Most good ideas don't appear as whole cloth (though this occasionally happens) but in slow stages, first as slight variations on known themes and then, as they develop, something new.

9. You'll think the good idea is humble

Good ideas are like newborn babies. They are fragile, though tough. They need cleaning up. The beauty is in its birth but also in the potential it represents. As the mother, you know what dream the idea may become, that it is totally dependent, that it takes time to develop, and that some day it will be incredible.

10. You've got to write it down

When you've actually picked up a good idea and hold it in your hand, avoid the temptation to set it aside for later. For a moment, you'll marvel at yourself for spotting it, and you will think, oh, I need to write that down. And then your mind will float back to a task. If you don't do something about it immediately, chances are the good idea will leave to find a more affable host.

Sometimes the tyranny of the task is unavoidable—trust me, I have four kids. I know. Yet I try as best as possible to cage the idea anyway. Next are five techniques I've developed to avoid the temptation to do it later.

How to Capture Good Ideas

One type of creativity is like a miner who has struck a gold vein and follows it to its end, regardless of how long it takes or how lost he gets. It's raw, unexpected, and beautiful. Another type is like a metallurgist who refines, polishing the raw ore into usable ingots. Both are legitimate ways to find good ideas. The first is the sexy version of creativity; the second is the realistic version.

Some days I have tapped a vein and just try to hang on. Most days I grind on the residue of pre-existing ore until I have created something usable. Since grinding is more common; the trick is always to have good supplies of raw ore.

Here's what I do to capture good ideas.

1. The microphone on my smartphone keypad

I use voice dictation on the afternoon commute home, when my mind is still in fifth gear. If something hits me, I'll talk into the keyboard microphone on a note-taking app, like this: "Write an appendix on creative tools period name five top tips period." The microphone converts the words and even spoken punctuation, resulting in complete sentences and a workable first draft.

Tip: If you're rushed, at least dictate two sentences about the idea, so you can build on it later.

2. My journal

I am part of the last analog generation. I like writing with pen and paper. I carry a journal most places I go and take notes as able. The reason I carry it is that I would otherwise end up with piles of scrap paper. The journal keeps it all in one place. I see journaling as a next evolution from the audio recording. It is good for doing a quick deep dive on a topic. If my mind has been off-roading on an idea for a while, and I have ten minutes to spare, I may locate a corner and pen a few thoughts, not as bullets or as a complete draft, but as a set of sentences that yields usable phrases on a new vein.

Tip: Carry your journal religiously. It only works if you have it with you. It's a habit you must form over time.

3. Organizing software

When I start collecting a series of ideas on a topic, in my journal or my phone or through bookmarked sites, I gather them together under one heading in an organizational app called Evernote. For example, I recently realized that I'd been brewing on a topic for several days and that whenever I talk to people about it, they respond enthusiastically. I created a notebook in Evernote, and made a list of individual entries for each separate thought I'd had on the topic. I made seven entries right away and added two more later that day. Later, I can go back and mull over the relationships of these ideas and look for connections and a possible future book outline.

Tip: Don't think of Evernote as your drafting software, but as a collection bin for an emerging idea.

4. Draft Software

When you sit down to create, you want to move fast and not be encumbered with bells and whistles. A lot of software has overhead to wade through; for drafting find a simpler solution. I do my first-draft writing in Text Edit or Pages for simplicity. Others recommend Scrivener or Google Docs. Whatever you use, you want simplicity and good backup.

Tip: Preset headings and frames so you can spend time on content instead of fritzing with style.

5. Professional software

When I'm ready to move to full drafts, I open up professional-level software. This is Word for a writer or Autocad for an engineer. People complain about Word because it's bloated, and it is. Don't use it for raw drafts, but only for finished products.

Tip: Think of the microphone dictation app and the journal as stage one, raw ideas; organizational software as stage two, groupings; and your professional app as stage three, the first draft.

Acknowledgments

We mythologize creativity as the work of the gifted few when, for the vast majority, creativity isn't romantic but a sustained and sometimes grueling discipline. Most of us are grinders who need editing, and I've had several fine readers and editors who have helped along the way.

Lil Copan supplied faith, seed conversations, and vital advocacy that any successful book requires.

Lauren Winner exemplified the Samuel Clemens aphorism that the difference between the right word and the wrong word is the difference between lightning and a lightning bug.

Michael Buckingham, Joe Carmichael, Mark Crumpler, Lori Fast, Gary Molander, Jim Ozier, Stephen Proctor, Hampton Ryan, and Wayne Wilson offered early reads and helpful feedback.

Several dozen blog readers at lenwilson.us, through the simple act of commenting, gave me the inspiration to sidestep the lies that threatened to steal my creative energy and derail this book.

Notes

Preface

1. Gallup, *State of the Global Workplace Report* (2013), www.gallup
.com/strategicconsulting/164735/state-global-workplace.aspx.

2. See www.ted.com/talks/ken_robinson_says_schools_kill_creativi
ty#t-795003.

3. E. P. Torrance, *The Torrance Tests of Creative Thinking: Norms-
Technical Manual Research Edition-Verbal Tests, Forms A and B-Figural
Tests, Forms A and B* (Princeton, NJ: Personnel Press, 1966).

4. Seth Godin, *The Icarus Deception: How High Will You Fly?* (New
York: Penguin, 2012), Kindle locations 943-947.

1. Trajectory

1. Brandon Griggs, "Could Moon Landings Have Been Faked? Some
Still Think So," CNN.com, July 17, 2009, www.cnn.com/2009/TECH
/space/07/17/moon.landing.hoax/.

2. Land's work appears in several publications and works in various
forms, most recently in a TED talk. See www.youtube.com/watch?v=ZfK
Mq-rYtnc.

3. Michelle Manetti, "UCLA's 'Life at Home in the Twenty-First
Century' Study Reveals Just How Disorganized American Homes Are,"
Huffington Post, www.huffingtonpost.com/2012/07/09/life-at-home-in
-the-twenty-first-century_n_1659172.html.

4. Dorothy L. Sayers, "Vocation in Work," in *A Christian Basis for the Post-War World*, ed. A. E. Baker (London: Christian Student Movement Press, 1942), 90.

5. Ken Robinson, *Out of Our Minds: Learning to Be Creative* (West Sussex, UK: Capstone, 2011), 13.

3. Wonder Free

1. Of the many sources I have studied about Twain, three have most influenced my account in this book: PBS, "American Experience— Biography: Samuel Langhorne Clemens, 1835–1910," www.pbs.org /wgbh/americanexperience/features/biography/grant-clemens/; Gary Scharnhorst, ed., *Twain in His Own Time: A Biographical Chronicle of His Life, Drawn from Recollections, Interviews, and Memoirs by Family, Friends, and Associates*, Writers in Their Own Time (Iowa City: University of Iowa Press, 2010); PBS, *Mark Twain* [motion picture], directed by Ken Burns, www.pbs.org/marktwain.

2. Bryan Goodwin, "Don't Wait Until 4th Grade to Address the Slump," *Educational Leadership* 68, no. 7 (April 2011): 88–89.

3. Steven Pressfield. *The War of Art: Break Through the Blocks and Win Your Inner Creative Battles* (New York: Black Irish Entertainment, 2012), 8.

4. Demons

1. Edison is mythologized for six thousand lone attempts at the light-bulb, and he helped perpetuate the myth of the lone warrior persevering against failure, when in reality his lab employed hundreds of assistants.

2. Pressfield, *War of Art*, 70.

3. Ed Catmull, *Creativity, Inc.: Overcoming the Unseen Forces That Stand in the Way of True Inspiration* (New York : Random House, 2014), 25.

5. Leaving Town

1. Stephen King, *On Writing* (New York: Simon and Schuster, 2000), 121.

2. Madeleine L'Engle, *Walking on Water: Reflections on Faith and Art* (New York: MacMillan, 1995), 81.

7. Heart

1. Kiona Smith-Strickland, "A Billboard That Condenses Water from Humidity," *Popular Mechanics*, April 25, 2013, www.popularmechan ics.com/science/environment/water/a-billboard-that-condenses-water -from-humidity-15393050.

2. Erin Bernhardt, e-mail conversation, October 14, 2013.

3. Ibid.

8. Soul

1. Walter Brueggemann, *Finally Comes the Poet: Daring Speech for Proclamation* (Minneapolis: Fortress Press, 1989), 109.

2. Makoto Fujimura, "What Do You Want to Make Today?" June 26, 2012, www.makotofujimura.com/writings/what-do-you-want-to-make -today/.

3. Victor Hugo, *Les Miserables* (New York: Thomas Y. Crowell, 1887). Kindle location 665.

4. King, *On Writing*, 47.

9. Mind

1. "The Galileo Project," http://galileo.rice.edu/sci/theories/coperni can_system.html.

2. Rob Siltanen, "The Real Story Behind Apple's 'Think Different' Campaign," Forbes.com, December 14, 2011, www.forbes.com/sites /onmarketing/2011/12/14/the-real-story-behind-apples-think-different -campaign/.

3. Ken Robinson, *Out of Our Minds: Learning to Be Creative* (West Sussex, UK: Capstone, 2011), 83.

4. Robinson, *Out of Our Minds*, 91.

5. James Lovelock, "How I Invented Electron Capture Detector," www .webofstories.com/play/james.lovelock/7.

6. J. E. Lovelock, "A Sensitive Detector for Gas Chromatography," *Journal of Chromatography A* 1 (1958): 35–46.

7. James Lovelock, "How I Invented Electron Capture Detector," www .webofstories.com/play/james.lovelock/7.

10. Strength

1. Martin Ford, "Productivity and Employment—A Structural Change?" *Econfuture: Robots, AI and Unemployment* (blog), June 7, 2001, http://econfuture.wordpress.com/2011/06/07/productivity-and-employ ment-a-structural-change/.

2. Gallup, *State of the Global Workplace Report*, 2013, www.gallup.com/ strategicconsulting/164735/state-global-workplace.aspx.

3. Robinson, *Out of Our Minds*, 14.

4. Steven Pressfield, "The Authentic Swing. Foolscap Video #1," www.stevenpressfield.com/blackirishbooks/the-authentic-swing /Steven-Pressfield_Foolscap-Video-1.pdf.

11. Blinking Cursor

1. "'Rocky Isn't Based on Me,' Says Stallone, 'But We Both Went the Distance,'" *New York Times*, November 1, 1976, www.nytimes.com/pack ages/html/movies/bestpictures/rocky-ar.html.

2. "I Am American Business: Julie Aigner-Clark," June 23, 2012, www.cnbc.com/id/100000488#.

3. Ibid.

4. "Talking with: Julie Aigner-Clark, Founder, The Baby Einstein Company," August 2000, www.bluesuitmom.com/career/womenbiz /babyeinstein.html#.

5. Seth Godin, "But I Don't Want to Do That, I Want to Do This," Seth's Blog, April 30, 2013, http://sethgodin.typepad.com/seths_blog/2013/04 /but-i-dont-want-to-do-that-i-want-to-do-this.html.

6. Daniel H. Pink, "What Kind of Genius Are You?" *Wired* 14, no. 7 (July 2006), www.wired.com/wired/archive/14.07/genius.html.

7. Malcolm Gladwell, *What the Dog Saw* (New York: Back Bay Books, 2009), 303.

8. Ibid., 302.

9. Paul Graham, "How to Do What You Love," January 2006, www.paulgraham.com/love.html.

10. Leonard Sweet's Facebook page, November 12, 2010.

12. Minecraft

1. George Plimpton, "Ernest Hemingway, the Art of Fiction No. 21," *The Paris Review* (1958).

2. L'Engle, *Walking on Water*, 23.

3. Brian Eno, Facebook post, January 26, 2013.

13. Half-Life

1. Charles Handy, *The Empty Raincoat: Making Sense of the Future* (London: Hutchison, 1994).

2. Brett L. Simmons, "The Sigmoid Curve and the Paradox of Change," June 5, 2009, www.bretlsimmons.com/2009-06/the-sigmoid-curve-and -the-paradox-of-change/.

3. "The Lesson of the Sigmoid Curve," *Dumb Little Man Tips for Life*, October 7, 2008, www.dumblittleman.com/2008/10/lesson-of-sigmoid -curve.html.

4. "Roy Campanella Stats," www.baseball-almanac.com/players/player .php?p=camparo01.